OTHERNESS
SOULS OF BROWN WOMEN

De.B. DUBOIS

ISBN: 9781522035695
First Edition

Author **De.B. DUBOIS**
The Girl Child (2015); Nandita (2016)

Edited by **AHANA BASU**
Senior Copy Editor of Pune Mirror
(Times of India)

Dear Readers,

More than a century ago (dated Feb. 1, 1903) *W.E.B. Du Bois* wrote in the foreword of his book, *The Souls of Black Folk:* *"Herein lie buried many things which if read with patience may show the strange meaning of being black here at the dawning of the Twentieth Century. This meaning is not without interest to you, Gentle Reader; for the problem of the Twentieth Century is the problem of the color line."*

Since then, the world has seen many changes, much war, many protests and ethnic clashes. So much so that we forgot what discernment, or rather discrimination, truly is. We forgot to appropriate devices of discrimination to modern equivalence. Even today, in the 21st century, many are discriminated against based on their skin colour, religion, country of origin, spoken language and even gender. In an ever-evolving world where billions of coloured folks, especially educated coloured women live and strive, this short read is intended to show what emancipation means to the coloured, especially to brown women. If at all a brown woman is included in this struggle for equality. In many ways, this book will sound like an appropriation and heavy adaptation of *The Souls of Black Folk*, and it truly is so. However this book is also a simple attempt to venture into deeper detail of how life can be for brown women – specifically of Indian origin – living in or outside their country of origin. Facing life in countries they've grown to call home.

Through this writing I wish to make clear the contemporary relations of the descendants of the non-coloured and the coloured in a 21st century context. Embracing this white world, I am stepping into the secret thoughts and daily lives of the brown women — here, I'll discuss the meaning of being the *"other"*, the passion of human sorrow, and the never-ending struggle for integration. These are true stories, real feelings, and honest sorrows of women of colour — specifically brown — who wish to remain anonymous. For them, I raise my voice.

Some of these stories have partially seen the light before in other forms: *The Girl Child* and *Nandita*. Complying with their republication, I thank Power Publishers, Kolikata Letter Press and Amazon. While to you, my dear readers, I shall say the same as *W.E.B. Du Bois* in his forethought – *I pray you receive my little book in all charity, studying my words with me, forgiving mistake and foible for sake of the faith and passion that is in me, and seeking the grain of truth hidden there.*

Yours truly,
De. B. Dubois

Jul. 18, 2017
Basel, Switzerland

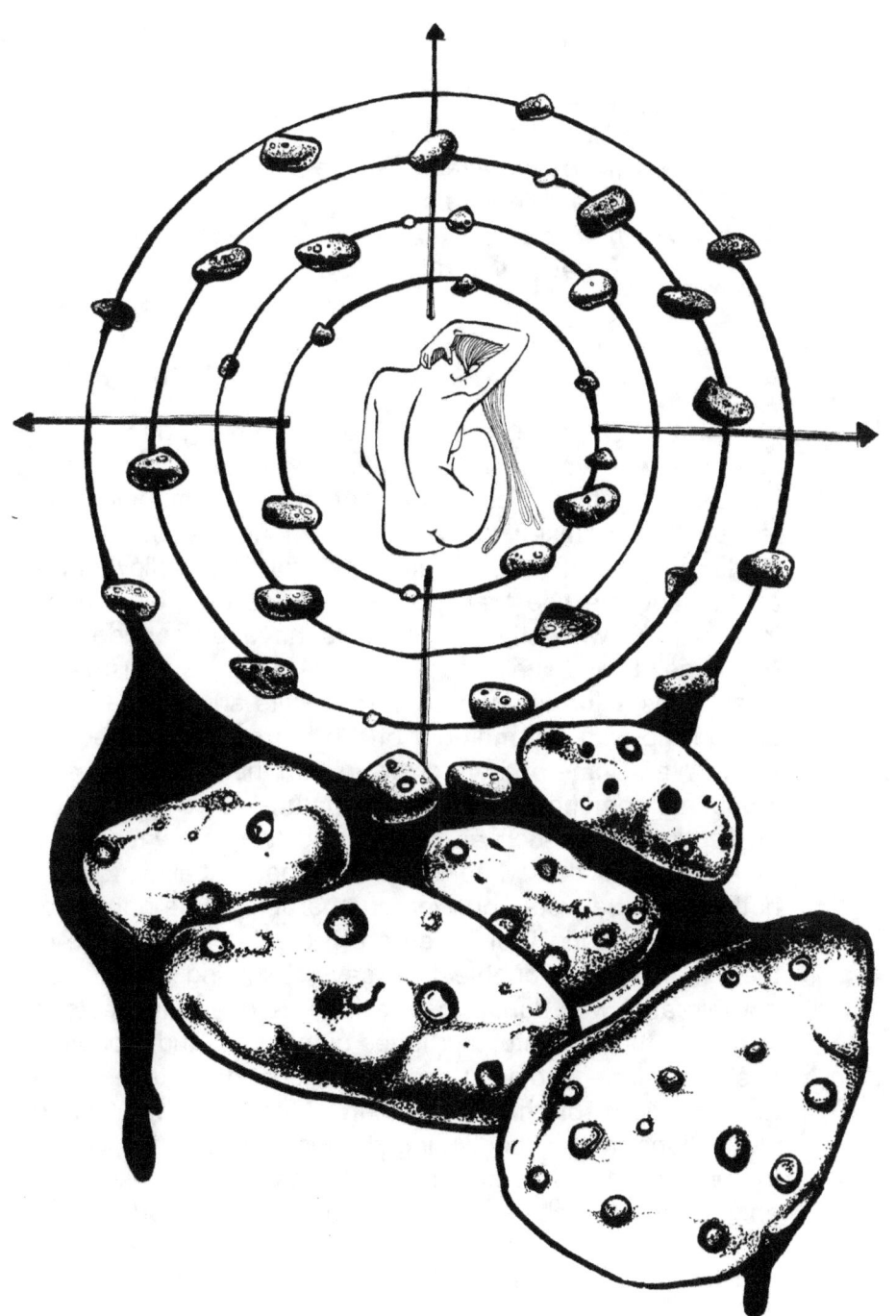

1.1

When I look into this world, there are hardly
any words not already spoken, there are
hardly any thoughts not already written.
Yet there are ears that need reaching and
eyes that need showing.

I live in the 21st century. A touchy world where, despite the fact that we live in civilised democratic societies, black souls are fighting a constant fight towards emancipation, red souls are limited to their government assigned native lands, brown souls are lost in translation, and yellow souls are fighting the tide that groups them as the new money trends – all while the white souls have proper identity. Germans, Swiss, Italians, French, Americans, Austrians, Australians – the list goes on. The white souls have been brought up with the memory of the horrors of the Second World War. Some of them grew up with the knowledge and it became somehow their "second nature" to be very aware of discrimination such as racism and fascism wherever it manifests. For the white souls are naïve believers that nothing can be worse or even comparable to the horrors of the Second World War. They are protected in a bubble of their making – a bubble that says, "Nothing can be as horrible as it was during the wars." This often manifests in forgetting those painful memories of wartime, and repeating mistakes that shouldn't be repeated: new time, new appropriations of the word "war." Most of the Western civilisations live in functioning democratic societies where the weapon of war is no longer physically deadly like guns and torture chambers. War weapons of our modern day society are words, body language and expressions. These can wound people deeply and even psychologically. Thus, amidst this world dominated by the white souls, and myself – a brown woman – there is forever an unasked question: unasked by those who are diplomatic and have a sense of elegance; while most people refrain from asking due to the difficulty of framing it correctly. All, nevertheless, try to find a way around it. They approach me in a half-hesitant sort of way. They eye me curiously or compassionately, and then instead of saying directly: "How does it feel to be a foreigner?", they phrase it in steps. 'Where do you come from? I know an excellent Indian restaurant in my town; or, I love Indian food; or, it is so colourful in India; or, such a beautiful culture; or, don't you miss home?' At these I smile, or am interested, or reduce the boiling to a simmer, as the occasion may require; to the real question, "how does it feel to be a foreigner?" I rarely reply.

And yet, being a foreigner is a strange experience, particularly for someone who has never been anything else. The *otherness* that goes with being foreign is something that has been a part of my experience even at childhood, in my country of origin. Apart from being brown – I am also a woman. It was in the early days of carefree childhood that the revelation occurred. Differentiation. I remember well when the burden of reality hit me. I was a little thing, wandering in the world of daydreams, with Misha comics open in front of me. My maternal grandmother came in with a bag full of wooden toys. At my grandfather's request, she handed me two and sat down to carefully pack the rest. When I asked her for one more from an array of about thirty wooden toys – she refused definitively, without even a glance towards me. When grandfather insisted – she replied "It's is for our son's daughter. Not our daughter's daughter." Grandfather nodded in agreement. Then it dawned upon me with certain suddenness that I was different. The *"other"* granddaughter shut out from their male dominated world by a vast curtain.

From then on, I had no desire to tear down the curtain, or to tiptoe around it. I kept my distance and watched over the years with fascination – how different I am or rather how different I was made to feel. I'd often get tired as this differentiation was not simply at home. Cultural capital and economic capital are certain things that define posh – particularly in a top-notch all girls' school. Especially when one's parents refuse to bring one up in a way that would turn one's head, and build one to be a nonsensical nincompoop ever so content about family history, daddy's monthly salary, mommy's wardrobe and potential bethrove. My days otherwise overshadowed, on rare occasions would turn brighter when I could answer a teacher's question perfectly, solve a math problem correctly, or get to walk around the school garden in peace – alone.

For most of the brown girls, it was all about being popular and being upfront and knowledgeable in pop-culture. Or, the brilliantly performing girls – it was about proving their worth at home, to be daddy's pride. Or *others,* who travelled to Europe and brought back goodies that they'd only share with the easily submissive fools, ready to follow these girls on the merit of foreign travels, provided by their hardworking parents. Throughout, in every brown girl, there was a common unspoken wish to be white. As their youth shrivelled into tasteless flattery, they developed into silent admiration of the pale world that they read about in books and watched on TV. Even the few Bollywood stars, despite their Indianness, were much paler than the average Indian population. Any gossip about them was tinged with awe of everything white; as these Brown souls wasted themself in a bitter cry, "Why did God make me so brown? How can I be white?" The gloom of the imprisonment within the four walls of our own desires closed round us, as we grew older. White walls everywhere – from soap advertisements to beauty products, from hair-care to washing powder. The beating hands of brown souls trying to scale the unscalable heights of whiteness would occasionally dirty those walls with honest criticism perceived negatively: an observation which soon groomed my reality. I am born long after the world wars, yet I am growing up in a world which yields me no true self-consciousness, but only lets me see myself through the revelation of the male and pale world: a world where my gender and colour makes me the *"other."*

This is a peculiar sensation – where this duality of gender and colour made me see myself through the eyes of the onlooker. Measuring my self-worth through the tape of a privileged world that looked at me with amused contempt and pity. Much more so as I moved out of my third world city of Calcutta – whose poverty did Mother Teresa jolt up a few notches to make famous. I confronted perceptions of the world where my *otherness* – that of a brown woman – remained reconciled. Brown. Woman. Two souls, two thoughts, and two ideals – trapped in one body, whose fierce strength alone keeps her from being torn asunder.

Despite being born in a 5000-year-old culture and civilisation – I often found myself being considered less than civilised. Surprising all with my table manners, my taste, my spoken English, learning ability and politeness. As much as it was a surprise, it was also an annoyance – for the white world attempts to negate brown civilisation and history. Brown history is the history of survival, a constant strife of surviving colonialism for over five hundred years. The brown world is neither strong like the sons and daughters of the night nor dominant like the children of the light – this dirty world is still savagely trying to survive exploits that left it hollow, crushed and confused: so confused that they worship the goddess Durga and yet makes sure a boy child is prized over a girl.

A brown woman is a product of this male dominant brown world. She is not advancing into the world to spread her colour; for there is so much that this world can learn from the unity of all the colours! A brown woman will not bleach her brown soul in a flood of white west, for she knows that her culture has a message for the world as much as every other culture does – a brown woman is simply getting out to the world for she has the opportunity to learn and teach, to have an opportunity to work, or simply be a homemaker as she stays a supportive partner for her brown man. However, there is one truth, she simply wishes to make it possible for other brown souls to be both Brown and Human. Without any repercussions from the crushing white walls and without having to worry about doors of opportunity being slammed shut in her face.

1.2

The motivation that drives a brown woman in this world is the hopeful optimism to be allowed as a co-worker in the realm of civilised democratic societies, to escape both the death and isolation of her native culture that anyhow treats her with *"otherness"*, to wife-partner-colleague or, to befriend and use her best knowledge, and her latent genius. For unlike the white souls, these brown women are taught to be docile, submissive, the honour of the family, a deity; basically that creature with the purpose of being put up on a pedestal. Therefore when a female tries to break free from these labels, this imprisonment through being put up on a pedestal, as imposed by the Indian society – they are often called names, derogatory in nature, inflicting shame. A faint lingering of the past where these same brown women were epitomes of intellectual and spiritual attainments, flicker a dilemma in their momentarily questioning minds; for to question any man is already her crime.

Here in Europe, in the few decades since the World Wars, the brown folks turning hither and thither in uncertain and cynical striving, which often made their very strength lose effectiveness – to seem like absence of power, absence of organisation, absence of focus – like dimness, or even to a certain extent, dim-wittedness. And yet, it is not dimness or dim-wittedness, this cynical striving is more like an inconsistency of double aims. The double-aimed struggle of brown people — on the one hand to escape the contempt of their country of origin by making enough money to send back home, and on the other hand struggling through white contempt for having the knowledge and skill-set that allows them to be hired in reputable establishments with well-paid positions. There are some who are highly liked by the white folk – these are the workers at petrol stations, kitchen hands, cleaning personnel, cashiers at grocery stores, ticket-sellers and the general poverty-stricken hordes working to make ends meet with half a heart due to their painstaking awareness of being the *"other,"* Some of these folk are highly educated – yet their educations remain unrecognised because their country of origin is considered inferior. The system is only made for the rich browns, who can start all over again and have means to fight – a willing family, and old money.

In all of these issues, the brown woman remains silent. In occasional cases where these women reach a certain status and class through relentless hard work, education and patience – her angry colleagues would bully her, pull her down, and discriminate her. Any angry outburst from her will only be counted and held against her. A brown woman is not given the divine right to question. As if it was not enough to face a world tempted toward quackery and demagogy, the criticism of both the white and brown worlds, toward her strong ideals would thus make her question her self-worth!

Words. Modern war weapon of words. I remember reading about the people of the Solomon Island. The power of words is such that instead of cutting down a tree, the inhabitants would gather around a tree trunk every day, chanting out their negativity through accusations, curses and derogation towards the tree. After a while, the tree would start to wane and eventually die. The psychology is the same with people, especially with coloured folks and brown women. Whether a brown woman is killed in her mother's womb, or killed during dowry harassment, burnt alive with her dead husband on his funeral pyre, brutally beaten up with charges of witchcraft or killed with words, anyone of a privileged position is a murderer when they destroy the potential of a brown woman's soul – a brown woman's life.

This apart, the western brown woman is confronted by paradox. The knowledge that her people are given a twice-told story appropriated and revised by her white compatriots, modified to befit their comfort. Absorbing that what is befitting to their bubble of happy privilege and ignoring the strife of these *"others"* and their *"otherness"* that cause them discomfort. The western brown woman are seeing their men not protesting, for these men travel in their brown groups – mixing with their Brown fraternity, partially understanding the implication of words spoken in quackery and demagogy; for these men have a great support, the silent wives who keep their homes straight, – happy and functioning, devoid of outside harassment. These simple, silent wives are often happy with the little that they get – the little pleasure of being able to take a walk alone down the streets of a western country at midnight without perils. The respect and envy of other brown women left back in their home country. Yet, there is a certain discontent. The western brown women, often being the educated women who followed orders and married according to what the family arranged – these women live with the knowledge that would teach the white world about her folks, and yet knows how incomprehensible and whitewashed the history of her own flesh and blood is. How much she is still expected to remain mute and blind, in the supposedly free world of the western lands. The melancholy of this felt paradox is what makes the souls of these brown women a beautiful abstraction.

Brown women have contributed greatly to science, and yet these powers of body and mind have in the past been strangely wasted, dispersed, or forgotten. The shadow of her past flits through the tales of the Vedic age, more than 1,500 years ago, where brown women were assigned a high place in society. These women shared equal standing with their male counterparts, had liberty that truly had societal sanctions and yet these liberties had loopholes that made sure these women were tamed. This dichotomy is seen with the ancient Hindu metaphysical perception of "Shakti"; the feminine principle of energy, multitasking and strength was consequent and synonymous with brown women of the Vedic age. This took the form of worship of the female idols by Hindus. Yet today, through history, the powers of brown women flash here and there like falling stars, and die before the world has rightly appraised their brightness.

Occasionally, there comes a rebel. A wife who wishes to express or a girl who wishes to articulate her innate love of harmony and beauty that set the rougher souls of her people alight in mockery. And yet, all of these issues manifest a good amount of confusion and doubt in the soul of the brown artist; for the beauty revealed to her was the soul-beauty of a race which her larger audience despised, and she could not articulate the message of her people – to her people of both western and eastern worlds. This waste of double aims, this seeking to satisfy two ideals that cannot be reconciled, has shaped a sad chaos within her, with the courage and faith and deeds of billions of her people — often wooing false gods and invoking false means of salvation, and at times, has even seemed adamant about making these brown women feel ashamed of themselves for normal human actions, such as endeavours to bring back the baton of light and knowledge to her brown folks.

The days of oppression are not over for these brown women, and some wish to see that one divine event that would culminate to the end of all doubts and disappointments; few races around the world ever had the courage to worship nonconformity with half such unquestioning faith as does the educated and self-dependent western brown women. To her, so far as she thought and dreamed, colonialism was indeed the sum of all villainies, the cause of all sorrow, the root of all prejudice; independence was the key to a promised land of sweeter beauty that ever stretched before the eyes of wearied Indians. Yet, incitement swelled one refrain – emancipation. In her tears and curses at all manner of gods, she implored to have freedom in her right hand and equality in her left. She is still waiting.

2.1

*A sense of belonging is that absolution one
needs to truly belong somewhere.
A sense of belonging is that absolution that
depends on welcoming language.
A sense of belonging is that absolution that is
not given out gently, but is a tiresome fight –
That some of us are still fighting.
A sense of belonging is that absolution, in
search for a loving home.*

Whatever good may have come in the years following World Wars and Indian Independence, the shadow of a deep disappointment rests upon the brown women. All the more bitter because the unattained ideal of a promised paradise – a promised land – with equal opportunities, with economic and cultural prowess was abundant save by the simple ignorance of common people. For the first few decades were merely a prolongation of the futile search for freedom, the boon that seemed ever barely to elude the grasp of Indians soon transformed to communal hate that took to streets: invading homes and butchering both Hindus and Muslims. The ghost of George Curzon's actions in 1905 (the division of Bengal Presidency into the Muslim-majority province of East Bengal and Assam, alongside the Hindu-majority province of the present-day Indian states of West Bengal, Bihar, Jharkhand and Odisha) is still haunting the brown existence. For that was the first blow, axing India into parts, dividing India into Hindus and Muslims: Hindustan and Pakistan. Thus flaming prejudices of far-right Hinduists, and angry Muslim Imams, culminated to restrict freedom of their collective brown women (Hindus and Muslims alike), while empowering their male folks. All these are maddening and misleading the brown folks over the lies of lazy political party representatives (often fuelling communal hate to keep their chairs), disorganisation of industry, and the inconsistent advice of friends and foes from outside the borders of the country, leaving the bewildered brown folks with no new motto beyond the old cry for freedom and paradise. Through all of this havoc, silent was, and still is, the brown woman.

As time went by, however, she began to grasp a new idea. The ideal of liberty and equality demanded for its attainment through powerful means, and her right to vote in 1935 had given her this. A voice. The ballot. She now regarded this device as the chief means of gaining and perfecting the liberty which fights for Indian Independence had partially bestowed upon her, by the same ballot upon which she had looked with the heightened hope and optimism of a visible sign of freedom. And why shouldn't she? Had not votes made and ended wars and emancipated millions in the West? Had not votes empowered the black freed folks? Brown women started with renewed zeal to vote in their nation. For somehow, within this chaos of looking out for the brown man, silently making their home a better place, while he chased after freedom for the country – she forgot her voice. He forgot her freedom.

With power comes responsibility. If the brown woman is powerful enough to vote, she has to be responsible enough to know right from wrong. She must be educated and opinionated. Not simply dependent on what the male folks relay. Thus she began to have a dim feeling that, to attain her place in the world, she must be herself, and not just the *"other"*. For the first time she sought to analyse the burden she bore upon her back, that dead weight of social degradation partially masked behind a half-named brown problem: jingoism and patriarchy. As a brown woman, she felt her poverty; without a coin to her name, without a home to her inheritance, without land, tools, or savings, she had entered into competition with the male, the rich, the landed, and the skilled of her society. She knows her worth, as traditionally, a brown woman does not own property, nor does she inherit if she has a male sibling, she is the property. She is taught to be meek and mild and undemanding. Directly or indirectly, a brown woman will grow up hearing these teachings hammered into her social conditioning:

- Women should be married by the age of 18, because by the time they are 25, they will become strong-willed, and one cannot 'tame' them.
- Girls should never leave their homes, and avoid by all means this evil Westernisation of women that makes women desire education and a career. "Is it really necessary for you to leave your homes, just for your ego and go chasing your career? Have we become so Westernised?"
- Shun vanity, or any object of vanity such as make-up and or avoid looking beautiful/presentable outside 'all natural.'
- Encouraging mothers to slap their daughters for looking into the mirror for too long, as it might develop their sense of identity.
- Dismiss any notion of gender equality. "Can you really hide your natural weakness or character as a woman?"

These are the bare bones of upbringing that a brown woman receives. This is what she tries to escape when she runs towards the West. Alas! To be a poor woman is hard, but to be a poor gender and a poor race in rich lands of dollars euros and francs is the very bottom and thus the epitome of hardship. The weight of her ignorance, not of the letters but of life, of business, of the humanities; the accumulated sloth and shirking and awkwardness of decades and centuries that shackled her hands and feet.

Her burden is beyond all poverty and ignorance. The red stain of lost family, destroyed lineage and heritage, centuries of systematic legal destruction that colonialism had stamped upon her race meant not only the loss of ancient Indian chastity, but also the hereditary weight of a mass of corruption from white omnipotence – threatening almost the obliteration of the aristocratic Indian homes, the lines of Indian royalty. So they did. Leaving the word "Maharaja" as nothing more than the butt-end of white jokes.

In the 21st century, this kind of shunning of a certain colour – that is not white – is called prejudice. Many explain it as the natural defence of civilised culture against barbarism, ignorance, purity against crime, and the differentiation of 'higher' against 'lower' races. To which, unlike the rest of the colours, the brown remains confused! Every colour and creed has the voice that comprehends so much of this strange prejudice that is founded on just homage to civilisation, culture, righteousness, and progress. To all of these, the western brown woman along with her folks would humbly bow and meekly obey. She stands helpless, dismayed, and nearly speechless before that nameless prejudice leaping beyond all of her racial and gender issues. That personal disrespect and scorn that she faces, the derision and systematic humiliation, the distortion of her lived facts to fit the comfort of the white souls and malevolent license of extravagance that is allowed to her just so that she can prove her financial worth, all these along with the constant sceptical ignoring of the optimistic future and the active welcoming of the worse that can come for people of her colour, an unspoken powerful desire to hammer-in disdain that the white folks have for everything brown – from Rabindranath (Bandyopadhyay) Tagore to dirt and stool — there rises a sickening despair that would disarm and discourage any nation and its people, save that brown woman to whom 'discouragement' is a constant tinnitus.

Facing such vast amounts of prejudice was bound to bring in the inevitable self-questioning, self-disparagement, and lowering of ideals which goes hand-in-hand with repression, thus breeding in an atmosphere of contempt and hate. Those brown women left back in the country are diseased and dying, their souls are tortured and tamed with unforgiving norms of gender discrimination; even to this day they cannot write more than their name, today their voting is in vain; what is the need for education, since these women must always cook and serve? Their nation, religion, culture echoed and enforced this self-criticism, saying: *Be content to be servants — housewives, mothers, sisters, and daughters — and nothing more; what need be of higher culture for those less than men?* The brown women living in the west — deemed evil and westernised by their own nation, religion, culture and deemed prudent by the uncomfortable white folks for these brown women speak up — out of the evil came something of good: careful adjustment of education to real life, clearer perception of their social responsibilities, and the sobering realisation of the meaning of progress; where their brownness must remain humbly concealed.

2.2

Similar to the 20th century, the problem of the 21st century is also that of the colour line. The relation between the various shades of darkness to the one dominant shade of light skin. This was the same problem that caused colonialism, exploitation of so-called simpletons, impoverishment of those exploited – the brown folks being reduced to dirt. Independence of India and Pakistan fixed the technical points, however the question of lost lineage, imposed disbursement of land owners based on lack of male heirs and partition of the country, loss of wealth and minerals –

and as we know, – that the question of unequal salary of the same brown folks when they landed with jobs in western countries of colonial heritage. Unequal treatment of the coloured – particularly brown-skinned – was and still is the real cause of the conflict. A 21st century conflict that did not involve guns when it came from the brown women, just a silent internal cry – where these women would keep their heads down and work harder. What the rest of the world puts a hundred percent effort to achieve, these women would have to put in two hundred percent or more – and still would be told that they are not good enough.

How many books have we read about the injustice towards the sons and daughters of the night? How many books have we read about the guilt that the West feels due to their actions? In comparison, how many books have we read about the struggles of brown folks and their brown women? The struggle of brown folks, and the injustice that goes hand in hand with everyday survival: these are stories that remain untold, unseen and unheard. For the brown-skinned are naturally submissive for they fear to be mocked due to their accent! Intentionally quiet, contributing to the progress of the world by making sure that their brownness is humbly concealed. Keeping their array of delicious food and vibrant colours under wraps – for they wish to make their way into people's hearts.

Curious it was, too, how this deeper question of *belonging* and *otherness* ever forced itself to the surface despite efforts and disclaimers by the white folks to keep this racket down, – started soon as the power of the British East India Company was transferred to the British Crown in 1857. There on, the Company, which commenced as early as in 1600 to build colonisation and trade, gradually imposed its rule in many parts of the Indian subcontinent, both economically and politically. Prior to the British, many parts of India were under the control of the Portuguese, the French, the Dutch and the Mughals. The Indian subcontinent was and still is a diverse culture, where their unity today is standing on the one soul struggle, – the struggle of identity, – to outshine their brownness that makes them the *others*. The mystical land that drew in rulers and conquerors of paler origins stands as a ruin where Indian culture and its people have lost value and identity. To the point that today, many brown folks are often asked a disturbing set of direct questions: "Does India have a history? Isn't it just stories and myths that pass on through word of mouth? Do you have a culture of writing and documenting history? Doesn't the history of India begin with the British?" To which many remain baffled. Such is the white wash over brown history of the Indian subcontinent, that the martyr for the freedom fight was also chosen by what suited the white taste: Mahatma Gandhi.

Many people have played significant roles in raising the national movement as their struggles lasted for decades, finally resulting in independence of the country. By remembering Gandhi alone, the west is negating all these efforts of freedom fighters, which played an extensive role in getting Indian Independence! An example: the *Revolt of 1857* was the first war fought towards the independence of India. The revolt started with the mutiny of the sepoys of the East India Company. The Muslim and the Hindu sepoys, together in unity, voiced their anger as the British introduced new Enfield rifles. To use these rifles, soldiers were required (quite literally) to bite the bullet. The paper cartridges encasing the gunpowder were heavily greased with tallow. This, the sepoys correctly suspected, contained traces of beef and pig fat. A strong example of disregard towards the values of both religions – where one cannot consume pork (Muslim) while the other cannot consume beef (Hindu). This disregard towards the *others* fighting for the same Queen is still the same problem in today's society – the neglect for their origins, their culture, their religion and their emotions that is associated with the same race – the colour brown.

This disregard for the brown goes beyond that. With a white-endorsed man, who had in one point shown contempt towards the black people, and wrote amicable letters to Hitler, while hiding his sexual exploits under the blatant lie of "experimenting with self control" as he initiated into further enslaving the brown women within the four walls of her home – one of the most singular and interesting of the attempts made by folks of many-a-great nations to grapple with vast problems of race and social conditions – the Mahatma. There too, it seemed obvious to the educated that this was no ordinary matter of temporary relief, but a national crisis. For, in one swipe, the white folks have refuted the struggles of Rani Lakshmibai, Mangal Pandey, Bahadur Shah Zafar, Nana Sahib, Tatya Tope and so on. These were some of the active leaders and freedom fighters that fought in the revolt and initiated the freedom fight, yet the world will only know Gandhi. Example: Mangal Pandey had played a pivotal role in beginning the revolt against the British. Despite his violence, without him neither Gandhi nor Nehru would have managed to steer their agendas for the freedom fight. As the men had played their roles, the modern world has forgotten the role of the brown women who fought side by side. Take Rani Lakshmibai: considered the symbol of resistance to the British rule and was one of the leading figures of the rebels in 1857. She rose up for her people, her identity – where she felt a sense of belonging – yet in colloquial language of her own native land, she is referring to as a taunt for *bossy young brown girls.* The only message it sends out to the young is that – it is scandalously wrong to ride horses and fight for one's own identity of being a brown woman.

Today, as these same brown girls advance towards the West, they are taken as threats. Their education, hard work and amicable qualities are questioned – yet these girls who turn to women in the western societies with naïve human compassion would overlook and forgive, for they are already grateful to walk down dingy alleys at midnight without fearing rape, acid-attacks and murder. However, many times these brown women are spat at in broad daylight, and yelled at by white strangers (go back to where you came from) empowered by their collective white cultural and economical capital of the country they know they belong to, these western brown women digest it all with the hope that one day this war against their gender and colour will be over. One day they will belong. The time will come when they'll be people again and not just brown women! For they can never be just Portuguese, French, Dutch, or just English, or whatever, they will always be brown women as well. But then, they'll want to be who they are. For the world and its inhabitants will love and respect humankind, and not just a privileged colour.

2.3

Three characteristic effects rose with the colonisation of the Indian subcontinent, which threw the brown situation of mystical colourful people in a faraway land, into the shadowy relief of Indian Independence: the Conqueror, the Conquered, and the Women. Some see only significance in the grim front of the destroyer, and some in the bitter sufferings of the partition. But to me, neither the conquerors nor the conquered speaks with so deep a meaning as that dark human cloud of hatred that clung like remorse to those swift changes intended to benefit the brown. Changes that benefit only the brown males, while leaving the women to figure out a way to survive. In vain were those fights for freedom, in vain were dreams of emancipation put into their deep big brown eyes; for no independence from the West can give these women the sense of belonging, identity, respect that their own folks cannot provide them with.

Indeed the pathological yearning for sons, and the irrational abhorrence to daughters, that drive India's characteristic traditional remedy is irrefutably embedded in the Hindu brown woman's ancestral ideologies: the Vedic texts. These are obsessively engrossed in the making of sons as a man's highest goal in life, because sons certify masculinity and immortality – sons endorse a place in heaven. Rita Banerji, in this fight for liberation of the brown women, wrote about this ancestral gift that Hindu women carry: *Likewise, they (the Vedic texts) hold women guilty of cheating men of this much coveted goal, and indeed being a serious threat to their (male) existence. Vedic texts speak frenziedly of women as "greedy" and "devious," like "wolves" and "jackals," who rob men of semen without giving them sons. Indeed daughters are seen as a woman's way of getting vicious with men. The texts regard menstrual blood as evil personified that can harm or kill a man. And so three thousand years on, menstruating women continue to be treated as pariah, or hauled to court like criminals. And many women who give birth to daughters are battered or killed.* Clearly, where does a Hindu brown woman belong if her own folks take her as an imminent threat to male existence? Where does she belong, if her own religion, culture, people are conditioned for 3000 years through the Vedas that actually sanctified the killing of infant girls and widows – transferred through generations in the form of hymns and religious rituals?

This is not simply the case of a Hindu brown woman, but also the youngest Nobel Prize laureate Malala Yousafzai. For standing up against the Taliban fatwa where girls shouldn't get educated, she was shot in an attempt to be killed by Islamist terrorist groups. Brown folks. These are our brown folks. There is no point denying that absolute truth. However, this particular murder attempt sparked a national and international outburst of encouragement for Yousafzai. Today, she is a brown girl who grew up to be a brown woman in the West. I cannot help but wonder: does she truly feel free and not confined? Does she truly feel a sense of belonging amidst the praises of the white walls that has shelved her on their highest racks – a pedestal? Does she feel the burden of the responsibility to act in a certain credible way – all the time, every day – even when she is perhaps hurting inside? For despite the praises and popularity, made even more prominent due to her work and her origins, she will always be a brown woman as well. Wishing for the many brown girls left behind that one day they would have a place, – liberated of all oppression towards women and girls, – where they shall truly find solace and a sense of belonging.

If we move our focus to the free country of India, there is one truth that we must consider: India is diverse. You can find almost every religion, alongside some hundred different languages and dialects that are spoken daily, vast topography, different shades of brown, different regional food and beverages, different ways of worshiping, different cultures – diversity. How can a country this big, with this many people have such common ground when it comes to respect for their women folk? Why are brown women silently tolerating injustice in their homeland? Why are they thankful for being in the West despite blatant discrimination? Gandhi. Amongst many other factors that unite Indians, the most important truth is that India is united under Gandhi. Long before Indian Independence, as a dissident in South Africa, he discovered a black youth, – a male, – harassing two of his female followers. Instead of taking actions against the harasser, Gandhi responded by personally cutting the girls' hair off. His justification for this action was that he did so to ensure the *sinner's eye* was *sterilised*. This matter was later boastfully scribed in his writings, where Gandhi purposefully pushed the message to all Indians that women should carry responsibility for sexual attacks upon them. This Gandhian legacy still lingers. In the summer of 2009, colleges in North India reacted to an outbreak of sexual harassment cases by banning brown women from wearing jeans, as Western-style dresses are too *provocative* for the males on campus. When such actions or measures against women are taken in the West, women respond by further questioning the system. However, in India, after a short-lived hullabaloo, the matter was eclipsed and everyone went back to the lifestyle of finding new ways to oppress brown women.

With the 2012 Delhi rape-case, more Gandhian beliefs came forward as Indians landed in debates over subconscious adhering to Gandhian beliefs. One such belief that Gandhi endorsed was that Indian women who were raped lost their value as human beings. Gandhi argued that fathers would be reasonable in killing daughters who had been sexually assaulted for the sake of family and community honour. Although, he moderated his views towards the end of his life, the damage was already done, as Gandhi's legacy lingers on, even in every present-day Indian press report of a rape victim – brown women – who commits suicide out of *shame*. Such is the nature of brown men, that in a 21st century setting, some would – much like Gandhi did – label Indian women using contraceptives as whores. However, one cannot singularly blame Gandhi for brown women's problems, neither can one omit the fact that the man on Indian banknotes, the father of the Indian nation (as is endorsed by many individuals in powerful positions of the West), fought and succeeded to ensure the country would never experience gender equality or freedom from indoctrination while his legend continues. A brown woman thus remains a creature, not a human.

I ask you this dear reader, where does such a woman belong? A woman who carries as a burden the very soul of her existence, where does she belong? Where is the absolution that a brown woman needs to truly belong somewhere?

3.1

*All your philosophy in one side, and all their
reality in the other – who do you think is
affected?
All your shame of a failed nation on one side,
and all their reality of not being accepted as
a national despite legal papers – who do you
think is more affected?*

In recent years there is a rising concept of Western Guilt. Which is described as a culture of remorse produced within the historic contexts of imperialism, black slavery and the Holocaust. In the American magazine of international relations – *Foreign Affairs* – the German-born American historian wrote (1987), that there is *"the rise of a guilty conscience in Europe"* as a *"major topic"*. All this is easy, but it is neither sensible nor just to bury the past by simply feeling guilty, as ever since 9/11 this same guilt finds justification in pointing out *"otherness"*.

Worrisome is the implication, when the same white world refuses to see a repetition of the said problem in 21st century settings. Yes, there are no concentration camps, yes there are no active colonial holdings of a Third World country – yet there is the hushed-up mentality of superiority, pride and ego. When faced with obvious instances of discrimination towards the brown, when faced with objecting to brown individuals growing up in the Western world – most white folks deny their actions by calling brown cries and protests as *goals overshot*. When Swiss psychoanalyst Carl Jung, wrote about German collective guilt in his essay of 1945, he asserted that the German people felt a collective guilt (*Kollektivschuld*) for the atrocities committed by their fellow countrymen. During 1945, however necessary it was to bring the Germans to recognise this guilt, in 21st century it is even more necessary to make them understand that atrocities in the form of hate speech and discrimination is still being committed by their current generation – born way after the World Wars. And by turning a blind eye, they are committing the same fault of not reacting before it is too late, – thus over and over again, history repeats itself.

And no, it is not simply a German problem. It is the problem of this current world. The century is that future which tries to forget and bury the past; and by doing so – repeating the same mistake made by their forefathers – slowly the world, in a collective whole, tips towards the far-right mentality. A far-right mentality consumed with a maximum of hate for the smallest of reasons, mostly directed towards the coloured: criminal aggression and heedless neglect towards brown existence. Through it all, amidst all these shades of dark to light in the west, are also the brown women.

3.2

What is this *otherness* one might ask. In sociology, '*otherness*' is central to the way in which majority and minority identities are constructed. These constructions of identities are due to the representation of different groups within societies – controlled by groups with greater political (and in some cases even racial) power. To understand otherness, one should also understand the ways in which social identities are constructed. These identities are not natural or innate. It is the conditioning that one receives while living within the structure of a society. That is, by living in a society that has been structured in a certain way, groups internalise established social categories within their societies, such as their cultural (or ethnic) identities, gender identities, and class identities. These social categories shape our ideas about who we think we are, how we want to be seen by others, and the groups to which we belong. As individuals within these societies we adjust our taste, our behaviour and our self-image based upon our interactions or communications with other individuals of the same society, including our self-reflection about these interactions. These give us an idea of being similar or dissimilar to the individuals or the groups that we interact with – thus furthering our understanding of where we stand as an individual in the given society, our identity and social belonging. Some identities have element of exclusivity. By adhering to a certain idea, or being able to identify with a certain group of people, we try to attain social membership, which depends upon fulfilling a set of criteria. These criteria, based upon which we attain social membership, are socially constructed. The sense of 'we' to 'them' and the sense of 'we' do not belong with 'them' for 'they' do not full fill our social criteria. This is the notion of *otherness*.

This notion of being the *other* highlights how societies create a sense of being-part-of an identity and social status by constructing social categories that put people within groups where they can relate. The problem lies with the dichotomies of *otherness*. Set up as being natural or normal. Often in everyday life, they are taken for granted and presumed to be natural – thus enforcing a norm around what certain societies see *otherness* as. But social identities are not natural, – they represent an established social structure, structured by the individuals living within the same society, – a hierarchy where certain groups are established as being superior to other groups. Individuals have the choice or means to be able to create their identities according to their own beliefs about the world – and find similar members of groups who have similar belief. Yet the negotiation of identity equally depends upon the negotiation of power relationships; where notions of superiority and inferiority are embedded in particular identities. The structuring structure of the society – i.e. the law, the media, education, religion and so on – hold the balance of power through representation of what is accepted as "normal" and what is considered as *other*. And visual representations of what is otherness have a special place within the social sanctions of cultural authorities. Example of which can be seen in our daily advertisements and media. In Western countries with a colonial history, like the UK, whether difference is portrayed positively or negatively, difference is always judged against the dominant group – namely white folks, middle-to-upper class heterosexual Christians, and cis-men being the default to which *others* are judged against.

When a brown woman finds herself in the West, such an institution of *otherness* is flung at her; with the best of intentions from the white folks being that the *others* can integrate themselves within the wide influences, great responsibilities, large control of wealth of the Western world – by actively learning the language and Western culture. This seems to develop a generally conspicuous position. Where enforcing a culture and a language on those who wish to simply live and let live, naturally opens up to repeated and bitter attacks from those who see (and are somehow threatened by) the positive possibility of the system. "What if these brown folks actually learn our language?" or, "What if they actually surpass us on the basis of intellect?" To these I have one answer: be confident.

On one hand, these unspoken norms of integration welcomes the *others,* yet simultaneously these structured norms pushes these *others* – away from 'paradise'. And by acting as a dominant White group, staying together against these *"others",* while using white privilege over these *others*, through action or inaction, for or against these brown souls, the white remain dominant. Whether or not those who exercise these privileges wrongly are aware of the success or consequences of their practices and whether or not the *others* are aware of the power being exercised over them – this is the devious nature of power play. Guilty are those, who – despite of having the privilege to stand-up for these brown souls, – would remain inactive and, question the motives of the dominated and underprivileged colours of the Western society.

The colour issue is such that despite compromise, war, and struggle, the brown is not free. I am confident in believing that by now many White readers would blatantly point out that I am enforcing a colour difference. *Otherness* is above and beyond colour. True. This painful repetition of the colour brown is to make one understand that not all critiques are simply critiques, just based on facts and not on people's race or skin colour. *But the hushing of the criticism of honest opponents is a dangerous thing. It leads some of the best of the critiques to unfortunate silence and paralysis of effort, and others to burst into speech so passionately and intemperately as to lose listeners. Honest and earnest criticism from those whose interests are most nearly touched, — criticism of writers by readers, — this is the soul of democracy and the safeguard of modern society.*

Based on the same ideals of *otherness,* often it is the honest criticism of a brown opponent that will be hushed. Leading to some of the best observers to turn in within themselves – refusing to share their opinion for to them it is an effort lost on a group who refuse to see logic and obviousness of situations. On behalf of whatever the reason, as long as the West teaches its children that difference is dangerous – *otherness* is dangerous – there will always be the colour problem. There will always be a silencing of honest critique. For even in the most cultured sections and cities of the white world, the brown-skinned are segregated servile castes; even today these browns are silently forced to live within communities where they feel accepted – a brown community. Even today, the Brown live with restricted rights and privileges. No matter what – the browns are the *others* who must integrate themselves, who must disappear and be invisible, mute and blind in a Western crowd where they are clearly unwelcome. In this *otherness* of being a Brown, further painful it is to be a brown woman — *this is the soul of democracy and the safeguard of modern Western society.*

As a brown woman I know the joy of being received as guest in foreign countries, the joy of being made a compatriot in a country where happy people know where they belong, rolling hills and snow-capped mountains stand as welcome committees sanctioning my day-dreams: dreams of acceptance and equal opportunities. And then, somewhere in this vast possibilities sits a veiled figure – whose dark glances rip out this brown soul – makes one realise how unwelcome the Brown are in this land of white possibilities. In the tainted air ruminates fear. "How do you people even get in here? How can people like you even make it within our borders? Who let you display your merit? You are nothing but brown dirt!" – questions I cannot answer. When I protest, Western Guilt makes lived experiences forgotten and invalid. These new children of the white, born long after the wars, advances while they unveil their dark human hearts, and now behold a century new for the dutiful repetition of old deeds: forgotten pasts! Children of the light stomp in and go on with the same shameful mistakes of their ancestors. Instead of remembering, instead of reminding, they claim to be sheltered from their horrific pasts. Then why repeat? This cowardice of not being able to accept one's past is ruining the future again, and again. Alas, again! The problem of the 21st century is the problem of the colour-line. The problem of the 21st century is the problem of the *otherness*. In it all – *who do you think is more affected?*

4.1

*Her cries are perceived and she is told she is
wrong. Her voice is heard yet it gets
suppressed. Her tears are seen and yet
questioned.
Her truth is called fiction, for no one walked
two steps in those flashing brown high heels.*

No matter what – be it black, red, brown, yellow or white –
all of us remain touchy about the sensitive subject of our
national history and culture. We remain touchy on the
subject of native languages, accents, teachings and most
importantly, colour. There is no escape. However, the only
good that can come out of any protest is first and foremost,
regaining respect. Showing that we are not mute, not blind
or incapable of knowing the difference between justice and
injustice, deaf or indifferent to what happens to us.
Unfortunately in this world, offence is still the best
defence. Thus to surpass this gendered and coloured
discrimination, we must exceed in individuality; first and
foremost, it is the duty of the brown women to be discerning
of their brown men as much as the society they live in (be it
in their land of origin or adopted nation), she must exercise
judgement. For the biggest weakness of brown women is
the fact that they do not judge their offenders. Instead, they
politely offer their other cheek when slapped. It is all noble
and beautiful as a gesture, but make no mistake – you'll be
slapped again and again and again: the slaps of a
collective society that discriminates against you, slaps of
unseen hands that never get tired!

The present generation of daughters from these spectrums
of colours are not responsible for the past wars that their

male ancestors waged, and they should not be blindly hated or blamed for it. Furthermore, to no gender is the obtuse endorsement of aversion in the recent course of the world as towards brown women! Where there is nothing more nauseating than to the best thought of their *safety*, – as the good willed intention of keeping them 'safe', – is the epitome of every injustice that is henceforth done to them. The problem with the brown man is that he'd rather look like a lion at home and a meek human outdoors – than be a lion for his family to the world and be a meek human at home!

Recently, in a forum against child sexual abuse, I came across a sentence that bothered me. I demanded that Indians must stop telling their girl child what she should or shouldn't do, and instead teach men and male children to not commit the act of rape. Why should it be the responsibility of a little girl to not sit on her uncles' lap? Why can it not be the responsibility of the grown-up uncle to not sexually-abuse the little girl who sat on his lap? By imposing that a little girl must not sit on her uncle's lap and have the awareness that she might get raped, is a way of imprisonment for the little girl and holding her responsible for any mishap that might happen to her. Instead, one should teach the adult male relatives to not abuse their nieces. One should give them a list of things that men shouldn't do to little girls or to little boys. It is not a child's fault. It is never their fault. To this a brown man replied – *"You seem to be totally confused. It is the girl who has to suffer for any wrong doing of male. Secondly whatever I have to teach I can teach my child only. I cannot roam around the world telling people how to behave with my child. Thirdly if I ask you to not let my child sit on your lap or do not touch her here or there how would you feel. What will be your reaction?"* Really? To his dim-witted reasoning, that matches the exact logic and attitude of many more Brown men, here is my answer: *"True, it is the girl who suffers, but she doesn't 'have to' suffer if the male relatives can behave themselves. Secondly, as a parent in a country where children, – be it a girl or a boy, – are not safe around male relatives, you will have to roam around the world (if necessary) telling your male friends and relatives that child sexual abuse is criminal and savage! For your child is not to be blamed if you are incapable of telling your male associates and family members that child sexual abuse is wrong. As a parent who couldn't make his child's surrounding a safe-haven, it will be your fault, – and your fault alone, – that you could not protect your child! Would it hurt, if as a father you tell your friends and family – "friend, try to understand the implications of such actions", or "brother, you are educated, must you make rape jokes and touch children improperly"? By that simple act, you as a brown man, you are making a change for the greater good that has respectable impact at home. In the process of such change if you lose such malignant acquaintances: good riddance! Thirdly, as for I, – if someone asks me not to let their child sit on my lap, I completely understand their concern and I will gladly oblige. That is called decency."*

It is this basic decency that the brown man must learn.

As for the brown women, they cannot be protected, as they are not safe if societies neglect their daily struggles. Their struggles muted and ignored only to give value where impoverished lands are in the uproar of social change, wherein all kinds of powers are fighting for supremacy; and to praise the evil, today the Western world is acting wrongly to condemn the good by involving in communal struggles. Yet, the one matter where they should lend their ear, the West remains deaf. Deaf to the loud cries coming from the souls of brown women.

Yet, it is the Brown women's discriminating and broad-minded criticism that the Western world needs the most, — for the sake of their own sons and daughters, and for the assurance of vigorous, healthy mental and moral development for future generations. But these brown women are silenced. For the remorse of a lingering

Western guilt is far more valuable than the honest critique of a brown woman. Today, even the attitude of the whites toward the brown is not the same; some ignorant Westerners from economically and culturally dominant lands hate the browns. The work force fear her competition, the money-makers wish to use her as a labourer, some of the educated see a menace in her upward development, while *others*, — blessed be the intelligent, hardworking *others*, the very few *others* amongst the same white nations, — wish to help her to rise. To these few *others* her soul cries out blessings, for these very few *others* make her struggles worth living.

4.2

Long time ago, when I was still an adolescent, – barely out of high school, – in a communal effort, some of us were called upon to volunteer to teach underprivileged children and brown women of a small locality of Calcutta. I was preparing for my A2 levels. Young and happy, I volunteered too, and I shall not soon forget that summer, some sixteen years ago.

Bright faces of housewives (homemakers), so many of them gathered around. Brown women with big wide brown eyes eagerly looking at us – waiting for us to speak. Some of them in their early twenties, just a few years older than I, already with five year olds in their laps. Some of them in their early 30s– reason for coming at our cause? *"Teach me. I want to learn. I want to be able to speak to my husband when he calls home from abroad. I want him to be proud."* These brown women, left behind, but their world is still revolving around the man their parents arranged for them to marry. Soon, I learnt from gossip (for my mother is mortally afraid of the brown man making his living in the West while his wife stays home in the East), that most of these brown men prefer having a domestic wife, while they toil in the West. To quench their appetites, they'd often have relationships with Western women – breaking it up when it becomes intense, with the pretext of "my family will never accept this". The untold part of the pretext of his story being, "my wife will never accept"! While the white woman hears – "my brown folks will never accept".

And so it was true. Slowly as the summer passed – most of these women could speak understandably and use computers to send their first letters to their beloved. The glee in their faces, the joy in their *"Hip, Hip, Hooray!"* as they congratulated each other, was the best reward any inexperienced teacher could ever get. Few days later, while walking down to the Metro station, one of my students approached me. Puffy eyes, her two-year-old daughter in her arms, her distress was palpable: *I did not learn English to understand messages from a white woman replying to my emails, instead of my husband. I did not learn English to know that we are nothing for him. How can I forget this evil language? Can't you take it away the way you gave it to me? I was better off without it!*
What could I say? That summer day I shall never forget. The soul of a brown woman was crushed. A mother, – a brown woman, – loathingly questioned education and a two-year-old daughter, – unknowingly in the long run, – perhaps lost a chance of advancement in a colour and gender dominated society.

I felt a deep weariness of heart and limb, as I boarded the Metro. I cursed men, from lands of varmints and cobras, their poisonous fangs dug deep into women of every culture. How can you blame the hate that will spew from there on, from a white woman in love, discovering that her brown lover has a wife at home? How can you ignore the cries of a brown woman who wishes to break free and yet is suppressed and told off by the society? The war weapons were no longer guns, but patriarchy toolboxes consisting of actions and words. That day, a brown man initiated a colour rivalry. By keeping silent and misusing his privilege, he was encouraging competition and divisiveness between two worlds already divided. By telling his wife to remain quiet in the face of such dire loss of trust, in perhaps ignoring communications from the mistress he created out of lust and boredom. If analysed carefully, this story could also stand true for similar actions from a white male towards his rightful family.

Equating masculinity with aggression, earnings, physical strength, dominance, – ignoring and devaluing men's ability to nurture, – and above all criticising opinionated and loud women. This is a war that many are still fighting. A war where the highest rates of casualties are felt by: brown women.

The ten years that follow youth, the years when first the realisation comes that life is leading somewhere, – these were the years that passed after I left my school. As I grew up in the West, I met more of these men. One set of rules for them and another for their women. I saw the same in various levels in other spectrums of colour – the only one I shall omit in this injustice is the white woman. Somehow, they have learnt to use the very tools of patriarchy that have been defined by men, against the same chauvinistic men. I envy them; – for despite it all, there are unsaid and hushed-up social sanctions that give these women more privileges. Their gender struggles are worth learning from. These women have made pioneering breakthroughs for the rights of women. These women defied norms and spoke up! Learn from them. Speak up!

Years later as I went back to visit India, I came by chance once more to the walls of my high school, to the halls of old memory. As I lingered there in the joy and pain of nostalgia, there swept over me a sudden longing to pass through the old Calcutta lanes, to take the Metro and to see the homes and the school of older days, and to learn how life had gone with my students. I went. Some old houses were gone, in their place stood new mansions. New cars driving by. I thought I saw a few familiar faces that I had taught. Older; and yet they were familiar. I remembered that summer of my adolescence.

Behind all its curiousness, I remembered the dim dangers of seeking knowledge, – confrontation with truth. How to some individuals, blissful ignorance shelter them from the world of bitter truth. If brown women remain sheltered, ignorant and fearful of reality, and if the world remains deaf to the voices of these women, if we refuse to educate and develop these brown women, we risk poverty and loss. You will never know if one of these women could have had answers to unknown mathematical problems or new formulas that could advance the world of science, art or technology. Even if we debase the race and gender factor, that has dug its fingernails into our mind and soul, selfishly sucking out happiness, blood and brain in the future to come as it did in the past, what can save us from decadence? Healthier self-regard can only be found in education, to help us see the right to all the wrongs of all our commotion and toil. To attain this, one must overcome fear of the unknown and have faith in humanity: give truth a chance over ignorance. Above all, stop putting obstacles in the way for brown women struggling to get a decent education; struggling to reach for their dreams!

4.3

We may decry the colour-prejudice of the West, yet it remains a heavy fact. We may decry the gender-prejudice of the collective world, yet it remains a heavy fact. Such curious twists of the human mind exist and must be considered sombrely. They cannot be laughed away.

Neither can a civilised democratic society successfully nor easily abolish all acts of discrimination by means of legislature. The act of discrimination by the 'privileged' needs attention! They must be criticised and stormed at. They must not be encouraged by being let alone while questioning the loud heart-breaking cries of brown women. They must be recognised as facts, unpleasant facts that need to be seen into, – as of the 21st century, this deafness, muteness, blindness towards discrimination is the very wall that stand in the way of civilisation and common decency, as it did in the 20th century. Why?

And so, in this great question of unification of vast and partially conflicting streams of thought, of race and gender, – the soul solution of education over ignorance leaps to mind. Not mindless learning of the letters and numbers, but harnessing such human training that will best use the labour of *all* without subjugating or dehumanising the *other*; such training as will give us poise to discourage racial and gender prejudices, and to stamp out those that in sheer outrage deafen us with the screech of prisoned masked souls, walking amongst us, constantly derailing us from decency, compassion and mutual understanding. But when we have vaguely said that education will set this complication of race and gender straight, what have we uttered but the truth? What can be more profitable for the world when no soul will be subjugated within the perils of gender, race and colour?

Remember.
Let us not forget our past, dear readers,
let us not forget the horrors that our
ancestors partook of.
No one in the future should be liable for
these mistakes, if only in our present we
persist on acknowledging their brutal
existence.

Protest.
Let the guilty hear you loud; let truth
resonate in their ears. Be brave. Face
these dire days, when human compassion
is mocked and ensnared: do not let
prejudice blind you.

Educate.
Do not let injustice done to the souls of
brown women go unheard and unpunished,
– do not let the coloured cry in vain, – if you
wish to reach for dignity, you must be brave
enough to face hell.

5.1 *Books*

My primary inspiration and influence has been W.E.B. Du Bois' *The Souls of Black Folk*; most instructional piece of literature that knows no parallel when it comes to summing up the struggle and pain of 20th century Americans of colour.

Anonymous, *The Pearl* (ISBN: 9780786702947)

Ariès,P., *Centuries of Childhood: A Social History of Family Life;* trans. By Robert Baldick (New York: Random House, Inc., 1962)

Banerji, Rita, *Sex and Power: Defining History, Shaping Societies* (Penguin Books, India, 2008)

Beauvoir, Simone (de), *The Second Sex* (London: Vintage, 1997)

Benjamin, Walter, *Illuminations*, trans. By Harry John (Harcourt Brace Jovanovich, Inc., 2007)

Berger, P., Luckmann, T., *The Social Construction of Reality: A Treatise on the Sociology of Knowledge* (London: Penguin, 1967)

Bergson, Henri, *Matter and Memory*, trans. By N.M. Paul and W.S. Palmer (Zone Books, New York, 2005)

Bilton T., Bonnett K., Jones P., Skinner D., Stanworth M., Webster A., Introductory Sociology (Palgrave Publication, 1996)

Blake, William, *Songs Of Innocence And Of Experience* (Dover Thrift Edition, 1995)

Bonnell, Victoria, *Iconography of Power: Soviet Political Posters Under Lenin and Stalin* (Berkeley: University of California Press, 1999)

Bourdieu, Pierre, *Distinction: A Social Critique of the Judgment of Taste*, trans. By Richard Nice (London: Routledge, 1984)

Bourdieu, Pierre, *Outline Of A Theory Of Practice*, trans. By Richard Nice (Cambridge University Press: 30th Ed., 2015)

Bourdieu, Pierre, *Language and Symbolic Power* (Cambridge: Polity Press, 1992)

Bourdieu, Pierre, *The Field of Cultural Productions: Essays on Art and Literature* (Cambridge: Polity Press, 1993)

Bourdieu, Pierre, *The Weight of the World: Social Suffering in Contemporary Society* (Cambridge: Polity, 1999)

Butler, Judith, *Gender Trouble: Feminism and the Subversion of Identity* (Routledge, 1990)

Clendinnen, Inga, *Reading the Holocaust* (Cambridge: Cambridge University Press, 1999)

Confino, Alon, *Germany as a Culture of Remembrance: Promises and Limits of Writing History* (The University of North Carolina Press: Chapel Hill, 2006)

Despentes, Virginie, *King Kong Theorie* (Grasset & Fasquelle, 2006)

DuBois, W.E.B., *The Souls of Black Folk* (ISBN-13: 978-0486280417)

Foucault, Michael, *Abnormal: Lectures at the Collège de France 1974-1975*, trans. By Grahm Burchell (New York: Picador, 2003)

Foucault, Michael, *The History of Sexuality, Vol 1: An Introduction*, trans. By Robert Hurley

(Vintage Books, 1990)

Foucault, Michael, *The Use of Pleasure, Vol 2: The History of Sexuality*, trans. By Robert Hurley (Vintage Books, 1990)

Foucault, Michael, *The Care of the Self, Vol 3: The History of Sexuality*, trans. By Robert Hurley (Vintage Books, 1990)

Frank, Anne M., *The Diary of a Young Girl* (ISBN: 978-0-670-91979-6)

Freud, Sigmund, 1948, *Civilisation and its Discontents* (London, Penguin Classics)

Freud, Sigmund, *On Narcissism: An Introduction, in On Metapsychology: The theory of Psychoanalysis* (Harmondsworth: Penguin 1984)

Freud, Sigmund, 1927, *'Fetishism', in On Sexuality: The three Essays on the Theory of Sexuality and Other Works* (London, Penguin Books 1977)

Freud, Sigmund, 1920, *Beyond the Pleasure Principle, in On Metapsychology: The theory of Psychoanalysis* (London, Penguin Books 1984)

Gudykunst, William B., *Theorizing About Intercultural Communication* (Sage Publications, Inc. 2005)

Hall, Stuart (edt.), *Representation: Cultural Representations and Signifying Practices* (The Open University, 1997)

hooks, bell, *Art on my Mind: Visual Politics* (New York: New Press, 1995)

hooks, bell, *Feminist Theory from Margin to Center* (South End Press, 1984)

hooks, bell, *Feminism is for Everybody: Passionate Politics* (South End Press, 2000)

hooks, bell, *Teaching to Transgress: Education as the Practice of Freedom* (Routledge, 1994)

Lacan, Jacques, *The Mirror Stage as Formative of the Function of the 'I'* (New York and London: Routledge, 1980)

Lacan, Jacques, *The Four Fundamental Concepts of Psychoanalysis*, ed. Jacques-Alain Miller, trans. Alan Sheridan (London, Penguin Books 1991)

Mulvey, Laura, *Death 24X a Second: Stillness and the Moving Image* (Reaktion Books: London, 2006)

Mulvey, Laura, "Visual Pleasure and Narrative Cinema." *Film Theory and Criticism: Introductory Readings*. (Edts.) Leo Braudy and Marshall Cohen. (New York: Oxford UP, 1999)

Narayan, M. K. V., *Flipside of Hindu Symbolism*, Jeanne Fowler, pp. 42–43, at Hinduism: Beliefs and Practices (Fultus Corporation: April, 2007)

Parker A., Russo M., Sommer D., Yaeger P., (edt.), *Nationalisms & Sexualities* (New York & London: Routledge, 1992)

Pacteau, Francette, *The Symptom of Beauty* (Harvard University Press: Cambridge Massachusetts, 1994)

Penny, Laurie, *Meat Market: Female Flesh under Capitalism* (ISBN: 978-1-84694-521-2)

Wex, Marianna, *'Lets Take Back Our Space': "Female" and "Male" Body Language as a Result of Patriarchal Structures*, trans. By Johanna Albert (Frauenliteraturverlag Hermine Fees, 1979)

Wolf, Naomi, *The Beauty Myth: How Images of Beauty Are Used Against Women* (London: Chatto & Windus, 1990)

5.2 *Articles*

To those who deny the fact of oppression of Indian brown women in their country of origin, here's a long list of newspaper articles collected over thirteen years. While the pattern of oppression was manifestly apparent, and the pattern remained unchanged over a decade, I found it traumatising to witness the high price of repression that went unchallenged by the ones repressed. In many instances indoctrinated brown women would further impose this act of repression on *other* brown women. Thus, the last article was collected on September 13, 2016.

Sep 13, 2016, Gujarat, India: Gujarat HC denies abortion plea of teenage rape victim. Indian Express.
http://indianexpress.com/article/cities/ahmedabad/gujarat-hc-junks-abortion-plea-of-teenage-rape-victim-3028172/

Sep 12, 2016, Uttar Pradesh, India: Mother, daughter raped in Uttar Pradesh.
http://www.deccanchronicle.com/nation/crime/120916/mother-daughter-raped-in-uttar-pradesh.html

Sep 12, 2016, Haryana, India: Woman and girl 'gang-raped as punishment for eating beef'.
http://www.telegraph.co.uk/news/2016/09/12/women-and-girl-gang-raped-as-punishment-for-eating-beef/ ; http://www.bbc.com/news/world-asia-india-37336050

Sep 12, 2016, Bankura, West Bengal, India: Acid attack injures three girls waiting for bus in India just days after landmark death sentence verdict.
http://www.abc.net.au/news/2016-09-13/indian-girls-injured-in-acid-attack-waiting-for-bus/7837536

Sep 11, 2016, New Delhi, India: Rape capital? No, Delhi is India's 'abduction capital'.
http://www.sakshipost.com/crime/2016/09/11/rape-capital-no-delhi-is-indias-abduction-capital

Sep 11, 2016, Coimbatore, India: '80-90% accused in crime cases go free'.
http://timesofindia.indiatimes.com/city/coimbatore/80-90-accused-in-crime-cases-go-free/articleshow/54272300.cms

Sep 9, 2016, Ahmadabad, India: Doctor 'held for raping dengue patient' in India.
http://www.bbc.com/news/world-asia-india-37320329

Sep 8, 2016, Thiruvananthapuram, India: India apex court seeks proof in Kerala rape-murder case.
http://gulfnews.com/news/asia/india/india-apex-court-seeks-proof-in-kerala-rape-murder-case-1.1893281

Sep 4, 2016, New Delhi, India: Former women's minister arrested for rape.
https://www.enca.com/world/former-womens-minister-arrested-for-rape

Sep 1, 2016, Kolkata, India: 2 Ola drivers held for rape-murder of Kolkata minor.
http://indianexpress.com/article/india/india-news-india/2-ola-drivers-held-for-rape-murder-of-kolkata-minor-3007205/

Aug 29, 2016, India: Female tourists should not wear skirts in India, says tourism minister.
https://www.theguardian.com/world/2016/aug/29/india-female-tourists-skirts-safety-advice; http://www.refinery29.com/2016/08/121558/indian-tourist-minister-women-skirts-safety

Aug 25, 2016, Haryana, India: Gang ransack house, kill couple, gang rape two female members of family, in Haryana.
http://www.americanbazaaronline.com/2016/08/25/gang-ransack-house-kill-couple-gang-rape-two-female-members-of-family-in-haryana416655/

Aug 22, 2016, New Delhi, India: JNU student allegedly raped by AISA activist.
http://indianexpress.com/article/cities/delhi/jnu-student-allegedly-raped-by-aisa-activist/

Aug 22, 2016, Haryana, India: Pregnant woman attacked by 3 men, gives birth to still-born.
http://www.business-standard.com/article/pti-stories/pregnant-woman-attacked-by-3-men-gives-birth-to-still-born-116082200008_1.html

Aug 22, 2016, New Delhi: Brother kills sister, police suspect sexual assault attempt.
http://www.newindianexpress.com/nation/Brother-kills-sister-police-suspect-sexual-assault-attempt/2016/08/21/article3590506.ece

Aug 21, 2016, Jharkhand, India: Uncle, nephew arrested for rape, murder of 4-year-old girl.
http://indianexpress.com/article/india/india-news-india/jharkhand-uncle-nephew-arrested-for-rape-murder-of-4-year-old-girl-2989162/

Aug 21, 2016, Maharashtra, India: Teacher held for sexually assaulting minor boy.
http://indiatoday.intoday.in/story/teacher-held-for-sexually-assaulting-minor-boy-in-maharashtra/1/745544.html

Aug 21, 2016, Kerala: Three years after her daughter's death at Kerala priest's residence, mother takes on Catholic church.
http://indianexpress.com/article/india/india-news-india/kerala-priest-arrest-fathima-sophia-father-arockiaraj-tamil-nadu-catholic-church-he-was-god-2987910/

Aug 15, 2016, Lucknow, India: She was raped at 13. Her case has been in India's courts for 11 years — and counting.
https://www.washingtonpost.com/world/asia_pacific/an-indian-gang-rape-victim-went-to-court-for-11-years-but-her-ordeal-continues/2016/08/15/c92075ce-5757-4073-b8c2-b0dc42f54ed0_story.html

Aug 13, 2016, Agra-Delhi highway, India: Woman's body found stuffed in suitcase, cops suspect rape-murder.
http://indianexpress.com/article/lucknow/womans-body-found-stuffed-in-suitcase-cops-suspect-rape-murder-2971817/

Aug 4, 2016, Delhi: Let women kill those who try to rape them: AAP Delhi minister.
http://indianexpress.com/article/india/india-news-india/let-women-kill-those-who-try-to-rape-them-aap-delhi-minister-2952392/

Jul 26, 2016, India: 14-year-old girl dies in second shocking double rape case in India.
http://edition.cnn.com/2016/07/26/asia/india-rape-cases/

Jul 25, 2016, Manali, India: Israeli woman allegedly gang-raped in Indian tourist town of Manali.
https://www.theguardian.com/world/2016/jul/25/israeli-woman-allegedly-gang-raped-in-indian-tourist-town-of-manali

Jul 19, 2016, India: Ahmednagar rape-murder: 'The men had nothing against us... in fact, I had saved them from goons 3 months back'.
http://indianexpress.com/article/india/india-news-india/ahmednagar-rape-murder-the-men-had-nothing-against-us-in-fact-i-had-saved-them-from-goons-3-months-back-2922702/

Jul 18, 2016, India: Indian woman gang-raped in 2013 is attacked again 'by same men'.
https://www.theguardian.com/world/2016/jul/18/indian-woman-gang-raped-in-2013-is-attacked-again-by-same-men

Jul 3, 2016, Hyderabad: 10-year-old raped, murdered by man recently released from jail.
http://indianexpress.com/article/india/india-news-india/hyderabad-10-year-old-raped-murdered-by-man-recently-relseased-from-jail/

Jul 1, 2016, Kochi, India: Kerala Dalit rape and murder: Accused charged for sexual activities with animal in separate case.
http://indianexpress.com/article/india/india-news-india/kerala-dalit-rape-and-murder-accused-charged-for-sexual-activities-with-animal-in-separate-case-2888269/

Jun 19, 2016, Muzaffarnagar: Woman 'raped', murdered in paper mill, two booked.
http://indianexpress.com/article/india/india-news-india/muzaffarnagar-woman-raped-murdered-in-paper-mill-two-booked-2861784/

May 5, 2016, India: Outcry in India over horrific rape and murder of 'untouchable' woman.
http://www.mirror.co.uk/news/world-news/outcry-india-over-horrific-rape-7905216

May 3, 2016, New Delhi, India: India in shock after brutal rape and murder of 'Untouchable' woman.
http://www.telegraph.co.uk/news/2016/05/03/india-in-shock-after-brutal-rape-and-murder-of-female-untouchabl/

Mar 8, 2016, Delhi: Girl, 15, raped and set on fire in India.
https://www.theguardian.com/world/2016/mar/08/girl-15-raped-set-fire-india

Feb 2, 2016, Berhampur, Odisha: Man arrested for raping a speech impaired girl in Odisha.
http://www.ndtv.com/india-news/man-arrested-for-raping-hearing-and-speech-impaired-girl-in-odisha-1272743

Feb 1, 2016, Jamshedpur: Rape survivor allegedly raped again at hospital.
http://www.ndtv.com/cities/rape-victim-undergoing-treatment-allegedly-raped-by-hospital-security-guard-1272207 ; http://www.aljazeera.com/news/2016/02/india-raped-minor-sexually-assaulted-hospital-160201134158908.html

Jan 30, 2016, Faridabad: Girl allegedly raped by 3 in Haryana.
http://www.ndtv.com/india-news/girl-allegedly-raped-by-3-in-haryana-1271853

Jan 20, 2016, Cooch Behar: Missing girl found hanging in West Bengal; locals allege rape, murder.
http://www.ndtv.com/india-news/missing-girl-found-hanging-in-west-bengal-locals-allege-rape-murder-1268050

Jan 15, 2016, Bundi, Rajasthan: 8-year-old tribal girl allegedly raped in Rajasthan.
http://www.ndtv.com/india-news/8-year-old-tribal-girl-allegedly-raped-in-rajasthan-1266382

Jan 14, 2016, Thane, Maharashtra: Teenage girl's road accident reveals rape, pregnancy in Maharashtra.
http://www.ndtv.com/others-news/teenage-girls-road-accident-reveals-rape-pregnancy-in-maharashtra-1265768

Jan 10, 2016, New Delhi: Raped, shot and thrown in a well to die; 13-year-old survives to fight back.
http://www.ndtv.com/india-news/raped-shot-and-left-to-die-13-year-old-survives-to-fight-back-1263969

Jan 9, 2016, Rohtak: Class 9 girl allegedly kidnapped, raped in car in Rohtak.
http://www.ndtv.com/others-news/class-9-girl-allegedly-kidnapped-raped-in-car-in-rohtak-1263891

Jan 7, 2016, Jamshedpur: 11-year-old raped, killed near Jamshedpur; complaint lodged after 6 days.
http://www.ndtv.com/cities/11-year-old-raped-killed-near-jamshedpur-complaint-lodged-after-6-days-1263019

Jan 5, 2016, Telangana: Teenage girl delivering baby in Hydrabad school washroom: accused arrested.
http://www.ndtv.com/telangana-news/teenage-girl-delivering-baby-in-hyderabad-school-washroom-accused-arrested-1262363

Dec 29, 2015, Kolkata: 14-year-old allegedly raped by army personnel on Howrah-Amritsar Express.
http://www.ndtv.com/kolkata-news/14-year-old-allegedly-raped-by-army-personnel-in-howrah-amritsar-express-1259988

Dec 15, 2015, Burdwan: 9-year-old dies after being allegedly raped in West Bengal's Burdwan.
http://www.ndtv.com/cities/9-year-old-dies-after-being-allegedly-raped-1255142

Dec 12, 2015, Delhi: Teen allegedly kidnapped on way to school, gang raped in car.
http://www.ndtv.com/delhi-news/school-girl-allegedly-kidnapped-raped-by-6-men-inside-car-in-delhi-1254002

Dec 7, 2015, Delhi: Minor allegedly raped, shot, thrown in well near Delhi; 3 detained.
http://www.ndtv.com/delhi-news/minor-allegedly-raped-shot-thrown-in-well-near-delhi-3-detained-1252181

Nov 23, 2015, Kolkata: Bengal police add rape charge after protests over girl's killing.
http://www.business-standard.com/article/news-ians/bengal-police-add-rape-charge-after-protests-over-girl-s-killing-115112300313_1.html

Oct 31, 2015, Gurdaspur: Woman commits suicide after dowry harassment.
http://www.business-standard.com/article/pti-stories/harassed-for-dowry-woman-commits-suicide-115103101247_1.html

Oct 13, 2015, Rajasthan: 85-year-old woman allegedly stripped and beaten with chains in Rajasthan.
http://www.ndtv.com/india-news/85-year-old-woman-allegedly-stripped-and-beaten-with-chains-in-rajasthan-1231636

Oct 12, 2015, Saharanpur: Woman set afire by husband, in-laws for dowry in UP.
http://timesofindia.indiatimes.com/india/Woman-set-afire-by-husband-in-laws-for-dowry-in-UP/articleshow/49328434.cms

Oct 6, 2015, Bangalore: Rape in India – Woman allegedly raped at knifepoint by private transport driver, cleaner in Bangalore.
http://www.ibtimes.com/rape-india-woman-allegedly-raped-knifepoint-private-transport-driver-cleaner-2128227

Sep 26, 2015, Visakhapatnam: 'Harassment' for dowry forces woman to end life.
http://www.thehindu.com/news/cities/Visakhapatnam/harassment-for-dowry-forces-woman-to-end-life/article7690691.ece

Sep 24, 2015, Mumbai: 12-year-old rape victim delivers baby.
http://www.freepressjournal.in/12-year-old-rape-victim-delivers-baby

Sep 8, 2015, New Delhi: ITBP constable accuses cop-husband, in-laws of assault, dowry torture.
http://indianexpress.com/article/cities/delhi/itbp-constable-accuses-cop-husband-in-laws-of-assault-dowry-torture/#sthash.2FuiUEga.dpuf

Sep 7, 2015, Mumbai: Monster dad knew he had AIDS, yet kept raping his daughters.
http://www.ndtv.com/mumbai-news/mumbai-monster-dad-knew-he-had-aids-but-kept-raping-his-daughters-1214904

Sep 7, 2015, Bhubaneswar: Parents of lady doc who jumped to death cry dowry torture.
http://odishasuntimes.com/2015/09/07/parents-of-lady-doc-who-jumped-to-death-allege-dowry-torture/

Sep 4, 2015, Chennai: 65-year-old children's home owner arrested for rape of 14-year-old.
http://www.dnaindia.com/india/report-chennai-65-year-old-children-s-home-owner-arrested-for-rape-of-14-year-old-2121830

Aug 31, 2015, JAMMU: An 18-year-old girl was found murdered after allegedly being raped in an open plot of land at Sainik colony area of Jammu district.
http://timesofindia.indiatimes.com/city/jammu/Girl-found-murdered-rape-suspected/articleshow/48738160.cms?from=mdr

Aug 30, 2015, HYDERABAD: A mentally-challenged minor girl was abducted, confined to a room and raped by two auto drivers at LB Nagar.
http://timesofindia.indiatimes.com/city/hyderabad/Mentally-ill-girl-gang-raped-in-Hyderabad/articleshow/48727583.cms

Aug 19, 2015, SHAHJAHANPUR, UP: Two brothers allegedly beheaded their 17-year-old sister over her relationship with a boy, and according to reports, paraded the severed head in their village.
http://www.ndtv.com/india-news/brothers-behead-teen-sister-march-around-village-with-head-in-up-village-1208749?site=full

Aug 17, 2015, Mumbai: Three-year-old raped by school van attendant.
http://www.hindustantimes.com/mumbai/mumbai-three-year-old-raped-by-school-van-attendant/article1-1381149.aspx

Aug 11, 2015, Chandigarh: Stalked and harassed, Punjab teenage girl immolates self, dies. In a video clip recorded by her brother before she succumbed, the girl, studying in class XI, has accused some boys from neighbouring Khandewal village of instigating the immolation.
http://indianexpress.com/article/cities/chandigarh/stalked-and-harassed-punjab-teenage-girl-immolates-self-dies/#sthash.0DcNQYmy.dpuf

Aug 11, 2015, Assam: A pregnant woman from Assam's Kokrajhar district has alleged that she was gangraped by two army men on Sunday night.
http://indiatoday.intoday.in/story/pregnant-woman-claims-gangrape-by-army-in-assam/1/457796.html

Aug 9, 2015, RANCHI: Five women were branded as witches and stripped and lynched in a village assembly at Kanjiya Maraitoli village under Mandar police station on the outskirts of the state capital in the intervening night of Friday and Saturday. The women were all in their 50s. Police identified the assailants and arrested 27 of them. Many of the arrested assailants are students of Mandar College.
http://timesofindia.indiatimes.com/city/ranchi/5-Jharkhand-women-lynched-in-midnight-witch-hunt/articleshow/48406526.cms?from=mdr

Aug 8, 2015, Gujarat: A rape victim who fell pregnant by her attacker and was refused an abortion by Gujarat High Court in India, is being made to balance a 40kg rock on her head in order to prove her purity and live with her husband again.
http://www.independent.co.uk/news/world/asia/rape-victim-made-to-balance-rock-on-her-head-to-prove-purity-in-india-10446759.html

Aug 7, 2015, Chaibasa: A 12-year-old tribal student girl's half-burnt body found, gang-rape suspected in Jharkhand.

http://zeenews.india.com/news/india/school-girls-half-burnt-body-found-gang-rape-suspected-in-jharkhand_1643554.html

Aug 3, 2015, HISAR: Parents kill 15-year-old girl, a case of suspected honour killing.
http://timesofindia.indiatimes.com/city/chandigarh/Parents-kill-15-year-old-girl-in-Hisar/articleshow/48322295.cms

Aug 3, 2015, Muzaffarnagar (UP): A woman constable was allegedly beaten to death by her husband and in-laws over dowry in Khatauli town.
http://www.tribuneindia.com/news/nation/woman-constable-killed-over-dowry-in-up/114968.html

Jul 30, 2015, Dhumaria: Woman killed by husband, in-laws for dowry.
http://www.business-standard.com/article/pti-stories/woman-killed-by-husband-in-laws-for-dowry-115073001348_1.html

Jul 30, 2015, COIMBATORE: Two unidentified men entered a private working women's hostel, on Tuesday afternoon and sexually harassed a girl.
http://timesofindia.indiatimes.com/city/coimbatore/2-men-enter-private-hostel-rape-woman/articleshow/48280624.cms

Jul 26, 2015, Ludhiana: A woman was strangled to death and her husband was brutally attacked by unidentified persons in the Shimlapuri area here last night. The woman's body was lying naked in the room. It is suspected that the assailants raped her before strangling her to death.
http://www.tribuneindia.com/news/ludhiana/woman-strangled-husband-attacked-at-shimlapuri/111430.html

Jul 25, 2015, Bangalore: Harassed for dowry, fiancée takes her life.
http://www.bangaloremirror.com/bangalore/crime/Harassed-for-dowry-fiance-takes-her-life/articleshow/48208645.cms

Jul 21, 2015, MUMBAI: A 15-year-old girl leaving for school on Monday morning was gagged and stabbed in the staircase of her building in Virar by a youth known to her and her family. The girl said that about a fortnight ago she went to the Manvelpada police chowkie to complain against the youth, who was stalking her, but was turned away (the police have denied this).
http://timesofindia.indiatimes.com/city/mumbai/Cops-turn-away-Virar-girl-stalker-stabs-her/articleshow/48152721.cms?from=mdr

Jul 20, 2015, GUWAHATI: A 63-year-old woman, who had been branded a witch, was dragged out of her home and taken to a nearby stream, where she was stripped naked and beheaded by a mob of nearly 200 people in Bhimajuli village of Assam's Sonitpur district.
http://www.ndtv.com/india-news/women-labelled-witch-beheaded-by-mob-in-assam-village-783453?site=full

Jul 20, 2015, BAREILLY: A 14-year-old Dalit girl was allegedly abducted and gang-raped.
http://m.timesofindia.com/city/bareilly/14-yr-old-Dalit-girl-gang-raped/articleshow/48148933.cms

Jul 19, 2015, VIJAYAWADA: A minor girl was reportedly subjected to sexual abuse by five youths at Bethleham Colony in Gunadala. The incident came to light on Saturday. Machavaram police took three of the accused into custody, and registered a case under section 376 of the IPC.
http://timesofindia.indiatimes.com/city/vijayawada/Minor-girl-in-Vijaywada-sexually-abused-3-held/articleshow/48132614.cms?from=mdr

Jul 19, 2015, Meerut: A 10-year-old girl was allegedly raped by her neighbour.
http://m.timesofindia.com/city/meerut/10-yr-old-girl-raped-by-
neighbour/articleshow/48136919.cms

Jul 18, 2015, Delhi: A 19-year-old girl died after being stabbed 35 times by two brothers who
had been stalking her for several years and against whom she had filed a police complaint
two years ago.
http://www.hindustantimes.com/newdelhi/delhi-woman-stabbed-35-times-dies-after-
protesting-sexual-harassment/article1-1370325.aspx

Jul 17, 2015, Etah (UP): Woman raped, assaulted by husband, brother-in-law.
http://wap.business-standard.com/article/pti-stories/woman-raped-assaulted-by-husband-
brother-in-law-115071700603_1.html

Jul 17, 2015, Agra: 10-year-old mentally-disabled girl, who was recovering after having her
leg amputated following a train accident, was allegedly raped at a Mathura hospital on the
intervening night of Wednesday and Thursday. Police have arrested one person in connection
with the attack while doctors believe that it was a gang rape.
http://timesofindia.indiatimes.com/india/Mentally-ill-10-year-old-girl-gang-raped-in-UP-
hospital/articleshow/48106979.cms

Jul 13, 2015, BHOPAL: A 23-year-old youth was arrested for rape and forcing abortion of his
cousin.
http://m.timesofindia.com/city/bhopal/Youth-rapes-Bhopals-minor-girl-forces-
abortion/articleshow/48052752.cms

Jul 11, 2015, Delhi: Drunk Delhi Police Assistant Sub-Inspector rapes woman. According to
the victim, the incident took place on Thursday night. The accused reportedly raped the
woman at gunpoint on Thursday and was also allegedly under the influence of alcohol.
Medical reports have confirmed the rape.
http://indiatoday.intoday.in/story/drunk-delhi-police-sub-inspector-rapes-
woman/1/450677.html

Jul 11, 2015, UP: A 23-year-old woman was allegedly beaten and throttled to death by her in-
laws over dowry.
http://wap.business-standard.com/article/pti-stories/woman-beaten-throttle-to-death-by-in-
laws-over-dowry-in-up-115071100717_1.html

Jul 09, 2015, Kerala: Couple held for using minor daughter for sex racket in Kerala. The girl
has told the police that her parents worked as pimps, who used to collect Rs 3,000 from the
customers.
http://indianexpress.com/article/india/india-others/kerala-police-bust-sex-racket-involving-
minor-girl-arrest-12/ - sthash.8rPwusJh.dpuf

Jul 9, 2015, VELLORE: Dowry Issue Tied to Woman's Suicide Pact with Son.
http://www.newindianexpress.com/states/tamil_nadu/Dowry-Issue-Tied-to-Womans-Suicide-
Pact-with-Son-Mom/2015/07/03/article2899024.ece

Jul 09, 2015, Lakhimpur Kheri, UP: Minor girl burnt alive in Uttar Pradesh, four men detained.
http://www.hindustantimes.com/india-news/minor-girl-burnt-alive-in-uttar-pradesh-four-men-
detained/article1-1367402.aspx

Jul 17, 2015, Agra: 10-year-old mentally-disabled girl, who was recovering after having her
leg amputated following a train accident, was allegedly raped at a Mathura hospital on the
intervening night of Wednesday and Thursday. Police have arrested one person in connection
with the attack while doctors believe that it was a gang rape.
http://timesofindia.indiatimes.com/india/Mentally-ill-10-year-old-girl-gang-raped-in-UP-
hospital/articleshow/48106979.cms

Jul 9, 2015, Bhopal: Terming it as a case of dowry harassment, the Sagar police have arrested the husband and father-in-law of Anamika Kushwaha, a trainee sub-inspector who allegedly committed suicide on Monday.
http://indianexpress.com/article/india/india-others/trainee-sub-inspectors-deathpolice-file-dowry-case-arrest-two/#sthash.i76tdook.yxZ0w8vc.dpuf ;
http://indianexpress.com/article/india/india-others/woman-cop-selected-in-exam-conducted-by-vyapam-found-dead-in-mp/

Jul 9, 2015, Shankar Nagar: A 30-year-old woman was found dead under mysterious circumstances at her in-laws' house. Her husband had been harassing her for a plot and Rs. 2 lakh, said the police.
http://m.thehindu.com/news/national/karnataka/woman-found-dead-family-alleges-murder-for-dowry/article7401836.ece

Jun 25, 2015, Indore: Dozens of women raped at Indian picnic spot in TWO YEAR campaign by ruthless gang who silenced victims and their boyfriends by recording the attacks and threatening to post the images online
- Gang would lie in wait for unsuspecting couples arriving at a beauty spot
- They would handcuff the man before taking it in turns to rape the woman
- In each case, they would film the attack and use it to blackmail the victims
- Suspect have reportedly admitted to raping 45 girls over a two-year period
http://www.dailymail.co.uk/news/article-3139150/Dozens-women-raped-Indian-picnic-spot-TWO-YEAR-campaign-ruthless-gang-silenced-victims-boyfriends-recording-ordeals-threatening-post-images-online.html#ixzz3lv93enMF

Jun 25, 2015, Muzzafarpur: 4 men attempted to rape a girl and shot at her two family members.
http://m.indiatvnews.com/news/india/youths-attempt-to-rape-girl-shoot-at-family-members-52033.html

Jun 25, 2015, Puducherry: Cousin attacks girl with knife for avoiding him.
http://m.timesofindia.com/city/puducherry/Cousin-attacks-girl-with-knife-for-avoiding-him/articleshow/47808646.cms

Jun 22, 2015, Chattisgarh: Nun, Sexually Assaulted in Central India.
http://www.ndtv.com/india-news/nun-in-central-india-is-sexually-assaulted-774151?site=full

Jun 22, 2015, Faridabad: Woman killed by in-laws through forceful intake of acid, for dowry.
http://zeenews.india.com/news/haryana/woman-killed-by-in-laws-over-dowry-in-faridabad_1618052.html

Jun 20, 2015, Gurgaon: Jobseeker gang-raped.
http://m.timesofindia.com/city/gurgaon/Jobseeker-gang-raped-in-Gurgaon/articleshow/47742054.cms

Jun 18, 2015, Ghaziabad: 25-Year-Old Pregnant Woman Killed by Husband and In-laws.
http://m.timesofindia.com/city/noida/Husband-in-laws-booked-for-pregnant-womans-death/articleshow/47722545.cms

Jun 16, 2015, Mumbai: Baby girl found abandoned in subway.
http://timesofindia.indiatimes.com/city/mumbai/Baby-girl-found-abandoned-in-subway/articleshow/47692467.cms?from=mdr

Jun 13, 2015, Kanpur: Minor girl set on fire for plucking mangoes in Fatehpur.
http://m.timesofindia.com/city/kanpur/Minor-girl-set-on-fire-for-plucking-mangoes-in-Fatehpur/articleshow/47656654.cms

Jun 12, 2015, Bengaluru: Bengaluru Amazon employee commits suicide after alleged dowry harassment.
http://indianexpress.com/article/india/india-others/bengaluru-amazon-employee-commits-suicide-after-alleged-dowry-harassment/

Jun 11, 2015, New Delhi: 13-year-old missing girl found raped and murdered.
http://m.timesofindia.com/city/delhi/Missing-girl-found-raped-and-murdered/articleshow/47621832.cms

Jun 10, 2015, Vadodara: Woman killed for allegedly practicing witchcraft in Gujarat; seven held.
http://zeenews.india.com/news/gujarat/woman-killed-for-practicing-witchcraft-in-gujarat-seven-held_1611043.html

Jun 5, 2015, Delhi: Woman gangraped by two sadhus at Meerut ashram.
http://indianexpress.com/article/india/india-others/delhi-woman-gangraped-by-two-sadhus-at-meerut-ashram/?SocialMedia

Jun 05, 2015, Jaunpur: Woman, 2 minor children burnt alive for 'dowry' in UP.
http://wap.business-standard.com/article/pti-stories/woman-2-minor-children-burnt-alive-for-dowry-in-up-115060500949_1.html

Jun 4, 2015, Panaji: Two Delhi women allegedly gangraped by five men, posing as cops, in Goa.
http://indianexpress.com/article/india/crime/five-men-gangrape-two-delhi-women-in-goa/

Jun 4, 2015, Faridabad: Man rapes married woman after saving her from committing suicide.
http://www.dnaindia.com/india/report-haryana-man-rapes-married-woman-after-saving-her-from-committing-suicide-2092443

Jun 2, 2015, Muzaffarnagar: Woman burnt alive by husband, in-laws for dowry in UP village.
http://zeenews.india.com/news/uttar-pradesh/woman-burnt-alive-by-husband-in-laws-for-dowry-in-up-village_1606066.html

Jun 1, 2015, Central-India: India tribal woman suspected of witchcraft, got gang-raped.
http://www.bbc.com/news/world-asia-india-32959841

May 31, 2015, New Delhi: Young Delhi lawyer fights off man who tried to rape her.
http://timesofindia.indiatimes.com/city/delhi/Young-Delhi-lawyer-fights-off-man-who-tried-to-rape-her/articleshow/47485605.cms?utm_source=twitter.com&utm_medium=referral&utm_campaign=timesofindia&from=mdr

May 30, 2015, Patna: Woman burnt alive for opposing husband's affair.
http://www.abplive.in/india/2015/05/30/article603995.ece/Woman-burnt-alive-for-opposing-husbands-affair

May 28, 2015, Chandigarh: Mother at 12, rape victim wants her baby adopted.
http://indianexpress.com/article/india/india-others/mother-at-12-rape-victim-wants-her-baby-adopted/

May 27, 2015, Rajkot: Four youths held allegedly for repeated rape of three minor girls in Gujarat.
http://indianexpress.com/article/india/gujarat/four-youths-held-for-repeated-rape-of-three-minor-girls-in-gujarat/

May 25, 2015, Barasat: Rape attempt on 67-year-old in Deganga.
http://m.timesofindia.com/city/kolkata/Rape-attempt-on-67-year-old-in-Deganga/articleshow/47409774.cms

May 24, 2015, Nainital: 23-year-old tortured to death for dowry.
http://m.timesofindia.com/city/dehradun/23-year-old-tortured-to-death-for-dowry/articleshow/47408523.cms

May 23, 2015, Faridabad: Woman allegedly raped by brother-in-law and harassed for dowry husband and in-laws.
http://indianexpress.com/article/india/india-others/woman-raped-by-brother-in-law-harassed-for-dowry-in-haryana/

May 18, 2015, Odisha: Woman, and her six-month-old daughter torched to death, by husband.
http://m.thehindu.com/news/national/other-states/woman-daughter-burnt-to-death-over-dowry/article7217392.ece/

May 18, 2015, Mumbai: Shanbaug, brutally raped by a wardboy in 1973, dies after 42 years in coma.
http://www.thehindu.com/news/cities/mumbai/after-42-years-in-coma-mumbai-nurse-aruna-shanbaug-dies/article7218651.ece?homepage=true; http://thelogicalindian.com/story-feed/exclusive/aruna-shanbaug-her-life-was-so-unbearable-that-we-are-happy-she-is-no-more/; http://www.firstpost.com/living/the-unbearable-agony-of-being-aruna-shanbaug-a-great-injustice-331622.html

May 18, 2015, New Delhi: Dragged out of an auto, woman kidnapped, gangraped by 6 men in Delhi.
http://www.deccanchronicle.com/150518/nation-crime/article/dragged-out-auto-woman-kidnapped-gangraped-6-men-delhi

May 18, 2015, Delhi Again: 26-Year-Old Woman Kidnapped & Gangraped By 5 Men, 4 Arrested.
http://www.tehelka.com/delhi-again-26-year-old-woman-kidnapped-gangraped-by-5-men-4-arrested/

May 17, 2015, Jharkhand: 14-year-old tribal girl kept chained allegedly by stepfather for 11 months.
http://www.hindustantimes.com/ranchi/jharkhand-14-year-old-tribal-girl-kept-chained-allegedly-by-stepfather-for-11-months/article1-1348202.aspx

May 17, 2015, Sambhal (UP): 22-year-old pregnant woman hanged by husband over dowry in UP.
http://m.firstpost.com/india/22-year-old-pregnant-woman-hanged-husband-dowry-2248530.html

May 15, 2015, India: I am not married, and I am single now: Anjali.
http://timesofindia.indiatimes.com/entertainment/tamil/movies/news/I-am-not-married-and-I-am-single-now-Anjali/articleshow/47282171.cms?intenttarget=no&utm_source=TOI_AShow_OBWidget&utm_medium=Int_Ref&utm_campaign=TOI_AShow

May 12, 2015, Raipur: Children burnt to death by man after unsuccessful attempt of rape on their aunt.
http://indianexpress.com/article/india/in-chhattisgarh-man-burns-children-to-death-after-woman-resists-rape/

May 09, 2015, Shirdi: Harassed for dowry, woman hangs self.
http://wap.business-standard.com/article/pti-stories/harassed-for-dowry-woman-hangs-self-115050900455_1.html

May 7, 2015, Gujarat: 16-year-old girl 'gang-raped' by five minor boys in Gujarat.
http://www.dnaindia.com/india/report-16-year-old-girl-gang-raped-by-five-minor-boys-in-gujarat-2084160

May 4, 2015, PATNA: Smita's dad charges her in-laws with murder for dowry.
http://m.timesofindia.com/city/patna/Smitas-dad-charges-her-in-laws-with-murder-for-dowry/articleshow/47153993.cms

May 1, 2015, Punjab: Day after death of 13-year-old girl, woman gangraped in Moga.
http://indiatoday.intoday.in/story/girl-gangraped-punjab-moga/1/433131.html

April 30, 2015, NEW DELHI: Marriage Sacred in India, So Marital Rape Does Not Apply: Government.
http://www.ndtv.com/india-news/marriage-sacred-in-india-so-marital-rape-does-not-apply-government-759219?site=full

April 26, 2015, New Delhi: 40-year-old woman gangraped in moving car in Meerut.
http://indiatoday.intoday.in/story/woman-gangraped-in-moving-car-in-meerut/1/432239.html

April 24, 2015, Mumbai: Mumbai Model, Allegedly Raped by Policemen, Texted Police Chief Rakesh Maria About Assault.
http://www.ndtv.com/mumbai-news/29-year-old-model-allegedly-raped-inside-police-post-in-mumbai-3-cops-arrested-757746?site=full

April 20, 2015, Mumbai: Nearly 40% deaths of Mumbai girls in last 5 years due to poor diet: CAG.
http://timesofindia.indiatimes.com/city/mumbai/Nearly-40-deaths-of-Mumbai-girls-in-last-5-years-due-to-poor-diet-CAG/articleshow/46980841.cms?utm_source=twitter.com&utm_medium=referral&utm_campaign=timesofindia

April 20, 2015, Bombay: Bombay HC rejects bail application of man in dowry, harassment case.
http://www.hindustantimes.com/mumbai/bombay-hc-rejects-bail-application-of-man-in-dowry-harassment-case/article1-1339141.aspx

April 19, 2015, Rajasthan: Woman Sarpanch, Sister Murdered Over Dowry Demands In Rajasthan.
http://m.indiatimes.com/news/india/women-sarpanch-sister-murdered-over-dowry-demands-in-rajasthan-232015.html

April 17, 2015, Ahmedabad, Gujarat: High Court says no to rape survivor's abortion plea.
http://m.timesofindia.com/india/HC-no-to-rape-survivors-abortion-plea/articleshow/46952101.cms

April 13, 2015, Chandigarh: Law undergraduates rape girl on Haryana University campus.
http://m.timesofindia.com/india/Law-undergraduates-rape-girl-on-Haryana-university-campus/articleshow/46901346.cms

April 12, 2015, Bengaluru: Woman ends life; kin allege torture by in-laws.
http://m.deccanherald.com/content/471316/woman-ends-life-kin-allege.html/

April 7, 2015, New Delhi: RBI top official gets bail in dowry death.
http://zeenews.india.com/news/delhi/rbi-top-official-gets-bail-in-dowry-death-case_1574967.html

April 1, 2015, Latur district: Suspected case of Sati in Latur, woman's body found from husband's funeral pyre.

http://indianexpress.com/article/india/india-others/suspected-case-of-sati-in-lathur-womans-body-found-from-husbands-funeral-pyre/

March 31, 2015, New Delhi: Delhi court says, minor beating by husband is not domestic violence.
http://timesofindia.indiatimes.com/india/Delhi-court-Minor-beating-by-husband-is-not-cruelty/articleshow/46751663.cms

March 29, 2015, Madurai: Madras HC acquits man who 'criticised' wife for being dark.
http://www.dnaindia.com/india/report-madras-hc-acquits-man-who-criticised-wife-for-being-dark-2072889

March 25, 2015, Baraut: Pregnant woman raped in Baraut, Uttar Pradesh.
http://www.dnaindia.com/india/report-pregnant-woman-raped-in-baraut-uttar-pradesh-2071812

March 15, 2015, Lucknow: Woman 'commits suicide' with three children, brother says 'killed for dowry'.
http://indianexpress.com/article/cities/lucknow/woman-commits-suicide-with-three-children-brother-says-killed-for-dowry/

March 10, 2015, Ranchi: 4-Month-Old Girl Thrown Out of Moving Train Survives.
http://www.ndtv.com/india-news/baby-girl-thrown-out-of-running-train-escapes-with-minor-injury-745516?site=full

March 5, 2015, New Delhi: Teen gang-raped in Haryana allegedly commits suicide.
http://www.ndtv.com/india-news/teen-gang-raped-in-haryana-allegedly-commits-suicide-744479

March 01, 2015, Muzaffarnagar: Woman drugged, gang-raped by five including cop's son in Muzaffarnagar.
http://m.hindustantimes.com/india-news/woman-drugged-gang-raped-by-five-including-cop-s-son-in-muzaffarnagar/article1-1321864.aspx

February 26, 2015, Dakshini Daulatpur: Woman beheaded, family members injured by relatives.
http://www.dnaindia.com/india/report-woman-beheaded-family-members-injured-by-relatives-2064409

February 25, 2015, South India: Indian factory workers trapped on promise of dowry.
http://dalje.com/en-world/indian-factory-workers-trapped-on-promise-of-dowry/537921

February 25, 2015, Sirsa: Alleging dowry torture, woman starts hunger strike against in-laws, police.
http://timesofindia.indiatimes.com/city/chandigarh/Alleging-dowry-torture-woman-starts-hunger-strike-against-in-laws-police/articleshow/46362977.cms

February 22, 2015, Kolkata: Goons molest woman, slit her throat.
http://kolkatainformer.com/5664/goons-molest-woman-slit-her-throat/

February 21, 2015, Bhubaneshwar: Odisha film director held for dowry torture.
http://odishasuntimes.com/114692/odisha-film-director-held-dowry-torture/

February 21, 2015, Delhi: Nigerian woman alleges gangrape in moving car, 4 held.
http://m.hindustantimes.com/newdelhi/nigerian-woman-allegedly-gangraped-in-south-delhi-4-held/article1-1319035.aspx

February 18, 2015, Gujarat: Father in India strangles his three young daughters because he feared wedding and dowry costs.

http://www.vancouverdesi.com/news/father-in-india-strangles-his-three-young-daughters-because-he-feared-wedding-and-dowry-costs/846941/

February 14, 2015, Baghpat: Baghpat 'cops' gang-rape 6 mths pregnant woman. http://m.timesofindia.com/city/meerut/Baghpat-cops-gang-rape-6-mths-pregnant-woman/articleshow/46238220.cms

February 10, 2015, Anantapur: Woman Beaten to Death, Burnt by Husband, In-laws. http://www.newindianexpress.com/states/andhra_pradesh/Woman-Beaten-to-Death-Burnt-by-Husband-In-laws/2015/02/10/article2661592.ece

February 9, 2015, India: Japanese woman accuses Indian tourist guide of drugging then raping her: police. http://mobile.abc.net.au/news/2015-02-09/japanese-tourist-claims-raped-by-guide-in-india/6081518

February 7, 2015, Chandigarh: Woman raped, brutalized and murdered in Rohtak. http://m.timesofindia.com/city/gurgaon/Woman-raped-brutalized-and-murdered-in-Rohtak/articleshow/46151730.cms

February 6, 2015, Bhojpur: Man guns down wife in train. http://wap.business-standard.com/article/pti-stories/man-guns-down-wife-in-train-115020601370_1.html

February 4, 2015, Bijnor: Husband, in-laws burn woman to death for dowry in Bijnor. http://m.timesofindia.com/city/meerut/Husband-in-laws-burn-woman-to-death-for-dowry-in-Bijnor/articleshow/46124737.cms

February 1, 2015, Kalyan: Woman sold off for Rs 1L, abused by 35 in a day. http://m.timesofindia.com/city/mumbai/Woman-sold-off-for-Rs-1L-abused-by-35-in-a-day/articleshow/46082994.cms

January 31, 2015, Madhya Pradesh: 11-yr-old girl beaten by policeman for riding his bicycle, sets herself on fire in Madhya Pradesh. http://www.dnaindia.com/india/report-11-yr-old-girl-beaten-by-cop-for-riding-his-bicycle-sets-herself-on-fire-in-madhya-pradesh-2057069

January 31, 2015, Madhubani: Three-year old found hanging on tree, rape suspected. http://ibnlive.in.com/news/bihar-threeyear-old-found-hanging-on-tree-rape-suspected/525892-3-232.html

January 29, 2015, Jaipur: Woman raped by driver, conductor in moving bus in Rajasthan. http://m.timesofindia.com/city/jaipur/Woman-raped-by-driver-conductor-in-moving-bus-in-Rajasthan/articleshow/46057669.cms?utm_source=twitter.com&utm_medium=referral&utm_campaign=timesofindia

January 25, 2015, Panchkula: New-born girl found on temple stairs. http://m.timesofindia.com/city/chandigarh/New-born-girl-found-on-temple-stairs/articleshow/46007021.cms

January 24, 2015, Lucknow: Woman poisoned for dowry. http://timesofindia.indiatimes.com/city/lucknow/Woman-poisoned-for-dowry/articleshow/45997641.cms

January 23, 2015, Haryana: 70 villages in Haryana has no girl child from the past several years – Maneka Gandhi. http://www.morningcable.com/home/top-stories/38995-70-villages-in-haryana-has-no-girl-child-from-the-past-several-years-maneka-gandhi.html

January 23, 2015, Vadodara: Gang of serial rapists busted: Confesses to 8 sexual assaults. http://timesofindia.indiatimes.com/city/vadodara/Gang-of-serial-rapists-busted-Confesses-to-8-sexual-assaults/articleshow/45985838.cms

January 23, 2015, Berhampur (Odisha): Girl raped in confinement, diploma engineer held suspect.
http://www.mid-day.com/articles/girl-raped-in-confinement-diploma-engineer-held/15937169

January 20, 2015, Ongole: Prakasam woman commits suicide in US, dowry harassment the cause? http://www.thehansindia.com/posts/index/2015-01-20/Prakasam-woman-commits-suicide-in-US-dowry-harassment-the-cause-126903

January 19, 2015, Bereilly: NRI husband demands Rs 1 crore from wife's family.
http://timesofindia.indiatimes.com/city/bareilly/NRI-husband-demands-Rs-1-crore-from-wifes-family/articleshow/45944781.cms

January 19, 2015, Varanasi: 65-year-old woman dies after being gang-raped, assaulted in UP.
http://m.timesofindia.com/india/65-year-old-woman-dies-after-being-gang-raped-assaulted-in-UP/articleshow/45942476.cms

January 18, 2015, Kanpur/Unnao: Woman chained to tree, set ablaze in Kanpur.
http://m.timesofindia.com/city/kanpur/Woman-chained-to-tree-set-ablaze-in-Kanpur/articleshow/45930732.cms

January 17, 2015, New Delhi: Man held for attempting to bury 9-year-old daughter alive in Tripura.
http://indiatoday.intoday.in/story/tripura-nine-year-old-girl-buried-alive-father-held/1/413818.html

January 17, 2015, West Bengal: Fresh incidence of acid attack.
http://www.newsx.com/regional/item/31988-india-news-latest-news-bengal-news-fresh-incident-of-acid-attack-reported-from-raiganj-west-bengal

January 16, 2015, Begumpur: Woman held captive and raped for ten days in UP.
http://www.dnaindia.com/india/report-woman-held-captive-and-raped-for-ten-days-in-up-2053055

January 16, 2015, Ahmedabad: Man who Claimed to Witness Girlfriend's Murder in Ahmedabad is the Killer, Say Police. http://www.ndtv.com/article/india/man-who-claimed-to-witness-girlfriend-s-murder-in-ahmedabad-is-the-killer-say-police-649756

January 15, 2015, Bhopal: Woman found murdered near farm in Bhopal.
http://timesofindia.indiatimes.com/city/bhopal/Woman-found-murdered-near-farm-in-Bhopal/articleshow/45897467.cms

January 15, 2015, Lucknow: Gangraped at 13, This Woman Has Been Waiting for Justice for a Decade.
http://www.ndtv.com/article/india/gangraped-at-13-this-woman-has-been-waiting-for-justice-for-a-decade-648831

January 12, 2015, India: India Doesn't Understand Its Rape Problem.
http://foreignpolicy.com/2015/01/12/india-rape-verma-delhi-modi/

January 12, 2015, New Delhi: 58 yr old woman robbed, murdered in Delhi.
http://zeenews.india.com/news/delhi/woman-robbed-murdered-in-delhi_1528737.html

January 12, 2015, Tiruchirapalli: Elderly woman attacked, robbed of two gold chains.
http://www.thehindu.com/news/cities/Tiruchirapalli/elderly-woman-attacked-robbed-of-two-

gold-chains/article6779347.ece

January 12, 2015, Uttar Pradesh: Indian teenager stoned to death by her father and brother because she loved somebody from the wrong village.
http://www.dailymail.co.uk/news/article-2906949/Indian-teenager-stoned-death-father-brother-loved-somebody-wrong-village.html#ixzz3RRlvuwxV

January 12, 2015, New Delhi: Delhi Woman Raped, Tortured, Strangled by Friend After Fight, Say Police.
http://www.ndtv.com/article/india/delhi-woman-raped-tortured-strangled-by-friend-after-fight-say-police-647386?site=classic

January 10, 2015, Delhi: Woman brutalised, murdered in south Delhi.
http://www.rediff.com/news/report/delhi-woman-found-dead-with-hands-legs-tied-cops-suspect-gang-rape/20150110.htm

January 6, 2015, Patna: Hunt for suspects after gang rape in India govt office.
http://www.channelnewsasia.com/news/asiapacific/hunt-for-suspects-after/1571904.html

January 4, 2015, Kolkata: Japanese Tourist Gang Raped In India.
http://uk.businessinsider.com/afp-five-arrested-in-india-over-japanese-tourist-gang-rape-2015-1?r=US

January 4, 2015, Delhi: India holds 5 in rape of Japanese woman.
http://the-japan-news.com/news/article/0001830144

January 4, 2015, Bodh Gaya: Indian brothers arrested over alleged kidnap and rape of Japanese student.
http://www.theguardian.com/world/2015/jan/03/indian-brothers-held-alleged-kidnap-rape-japanese-student

January 4, 2015, West Bengal: Son kills mother in a fit of rage.
http://timesofindia.indiatimes.com/city/kolkata/Son-kills-mother-in-a-fit-of-rage/articleshow/45745760.cms

January 3, 2015, Guntur: Man tries to cut infant son's hand inorder-to pressurise wife to pay dowry. http://www.deccanchronicle.com/150103/nation-crime/article/man-tries-cut-son's-hand-dowry

January 3, 2015, Bihar: Woman's tongue cut off for defecating in field.
http://www.deccanchronicle.com/150103/nation-crime/article/womans-tongue-cut-defecating-field

January 2, 2015, India: 22-Year-Old Woman in India Gang Raped and Forced to Have Abortion.
http://www.lifenews.com/2015/01/02/22-year-old-woman-in-india-gang-raped-and-forced-to-have-abortion/

Dec 31, 2014, SURAT: Ex-boyfriend shares photo on web, woman's body shamed, thus girl's engagement cancelled.
http://m.timesofindia.com/articleshow/45695510.cms

Dec 24, 2014, Rajasthan: Caste court wants rape-victim's nose cut-off.
http://www.hindustantimes.com/india-news/jaipur/caste-panchayat-orders-nose-of-dalit-rape-victim-chopped-off/article1-1299716.aspx

Dec 23, 2014, Delhi: Miscreants throw acid on a woman doctor, victim admitted to AIIMS
http://m.ibnlive.com/news/delhi-miscreants-throw-acid-on-a-woman-doctor-victim-admitted-to-aiims/519510-3-244.html

Dec 22, 2014, Puducherry: Two arrested for raping Aurobindo Ashram evictee
http://m.thehindu.com/news/cities/puducherry/two-arrested-for-raping-aurobindo-ashram-evictee/article6716149.ece/

Dec 20, 2014, Gurdaspur (Punjab): Minor girl raped, strangulated to death in Punjab
http://www.dnaindia.com/india/report-minor-girl-raped-strangulated-to-death-in-punjab-2045755

Dec 20, 2014, New Delhi: Girl gangraped by two friends in Delhi on her birthday
http://indiatoday.intoday.in/story/girl-gangraped-by-friends-in-delhi-sexual-assault-gangrape/1/408047.html

Dec 15, 2014, Patna: 65-year-old commits 'sati' in Bihar.
http://m.timesofindia.com/india/65-year-old-commits-sati-in-Bihar/articleshow/45517308.cms

Dec 13, 2014, Delhi: Airport employee beaten up and arrested for molesting 40-years-old flier
http://www.hindustantimes.com/india-news/newdelhi/delhi-airport-employee-beaten-up-arrested-for-molesting-40-year-old-flier/article1-1296083.aspx

Dec 11, 2014, Srinagar: Law Student Attacked With Acid By Unknown Person in Srinagar
http://www.ndtv.com/article/cities/law-student-attacked-with-acid-by-unknown-person-in-srinagar-633044?site=classic

Dec 11, 2014, NEW DELHI: 12-Year-Old Girl Allegedly Murdered in Delhi's Jahangirpuri Area
http://www.ndtv.com/article/cities/12-year-old-girl-allegedly-murdered-in-delhi-s-jahangirpuri-area-632839?site=classic

Dec 10, 2014, Ludhiana: Policemen Suspended After Woman Is Burnt By Her Alleged Rapists in Ludhiana
http://www.ndtv.com/article/cities/policemen-suspended-after-woman-is-burnt-by-her-alleged-rapists-in-ludhiana-632450?site=classic

Dec 10, 2014, Panvel: Pregnant woman beaten to death for dowry
http://www.dnaindia.com/mumbai/report-panvel-pregnant-woman-beaten-to-death-for-dowry-2042595

Dec 8, 2014, VIJAYAWADA: Andhra Teen Died After 3 Abortions, Teachers Arrested
http://www.ndtv.com/article/south/andhra-teen-died-after-3-abortions-teachers-arrested-631418?site=classic

Dec 8, 2014, Ahmedabad: Woman raped inside public toilet by attendant
http://www.dnaindia.com/india/report-ahmedabad-woman-raped-inside-public-toilet-by-attendant-2042007

Dec 7, 2014, NEW DELHI: Woman Accuses Uber Driver in India of Rape
http://mobile.nytimes.com/2014/12/08/world/asia/woman-accuses-uber-driver-in-india-of-rape.html?_r=2&referrer=

Dec 6, 2014, RAIPUR: 210 women tortured to death for 'witchcraft' in Chhattisgarh, many await justice.
http://m.timesofindia.com/india/210-women-tortured-to-death-for-witchcraft-in-Chhattisgarh-many-await-justice/articleshow/45397113.cms

Dec 06, 2014, KOLKATA: Viswa Bharati Schoolgirl Alleges Rape by PhD Scholar, Accused Arrested.
http://www.ndtv.com/article/india/viswa-bharati-schoolgirl-alleges-rape-by-phd-scholar-accused-arrested-630875?site=classic

Dec 06, 2014, CANNING, WEST BENGAL: Father Allegedly Slashed Daughter's Tongue For Having Affair in West Bengal.
http://www.ndtv.com/article/india/father-allegedly-slashed-daughter-s-tongue-for-having-affair-in-west-bengal-630914?site=classic

Dec 5, 2014, HYDERABAD: Fed up with additional dowry demands, woman drowns daughters, self.
http://m.timesofindia.com/city/hyderabad/Fed-up-with-additional-dowry-demands-woman-drowns-daughters-self/articleshow/45378871.cms

Dec 4, 2014, Delhi: Kerala girl repeatedly raped, held captive for a month by acquaintance in Delhi.
http://indiatoday.intoday.in/story/kerala-girl-repeatedly-raped-held-captive-for-a-month-by-acquaintance-in-delhi/1/405034.html

Dec 3, 2014, Gujarat: 6-month-old raped in Gujarat.
http://m.thehindu.com/news/national/6monthold-raped-in-gujarat/article6659025.ece/

Nov 30, 2014, Hapur: Hindu Man, Muslim Wife Hacked to Death in Broad Daylight in Hapur
http://www.ndtv.com/article/india/hindu-man-muslim-wife-hacked-to-death-in-broad-daylight-in-hapur-627786?site=classic

Nov 28, 2014, BAREILLY: Woman councillor attacked with acid.
http://m.timesofindia.com/city/bareilly/Woman-councillor-attacked-with-acid/articleshow/45311667.cms

Nov 28, 2014, Hisar: Rape victim delivers stillborn baby.
http://www.tribuneindia.com/2014/20141129/haryana.htm#13

Nov 26, 2014, NAVI MUMBAI: Man, mother beat pregnant wife over dowry in Koparkhairane
http://m.timesofindia.com/city/navi-mumbai/Man-mother-beat-pregnant-wife-over-dowry-in-Koparkhairane/articleshow/45275092.cms

Nov 24, 2014, NEW DELHI: Husband Gets 10 years in Jail for Abetting Rape of Wife
http://www.ndtv.com/article/cities/husband-gets-10-years-in-jail-for-abetting-rape-of-wife-625215?site=classic

Nov 23, 2014, RAIPUR: Branded witch, 2 battered to death in Narayanpur
http://timesofindia.indiatimes.com/city/raipur/Branded-witch-2-battered-to-death-in-Narayanpur/articleshow/45244446.cms

Nov 22, 2014, Mumbai: No help for 8-yr-old rape victim.
http://www.dnaindia.com/mumbai/report-no-help-for-8-yr-old-rape-victim-2037381

Nov 21, 2014, SURAT: Woman accuses six of raping her thrice in five hours in Surat
http://m.timesofindia.com/city/surat/Woman-accuses-six-of-raping-her-thrice-in-five-hours-in-Surat/articleshow/45224454.cms

Nov 2, 2014, Itanagar: Woman raped & murdered in Arunachal.
http://m.timesofindia.com/city/guwahati/Woman-raped-murdered-in-Arunachal/articleshow/45007771.cms

Nov 1, 2014, India: Female infant abandoned at Government Hospital in Krishnagiri
http://m.thehindu.com/news/national/tamil-nadu/female-infant-abandoned-at-government-hospital-in-krishnagiri/article6555086.ece/

Oct 31, 2014, BANGALORE: Bangalore's shame: 6-year-old girl raped twice by teacher on school campus.

http://m.timesofindia.com/city/bangalore/Bangalores-shame-6-year-old-girl-raped-twice-by-teacher-on-school-campus/articleshow/44988308.cms?utm_source=facebook.com&utm_medium=referral&utm_campaign=TOI

Oct 30, 2014, SURAT: Man threatens to circulate private video of wife for dowry, arrested
http://m.timesofindia.com/City/Surat/Man-threatens-to-circulate-private-video-of-wife-for-dowry-arrested/articleshow/44984672.cms

October 27, 2014, Raipur: On suspicion of 'witchcraft', woman stripped, killed in public
http://indianexpress.com/article/india/india-others/on-suspicion-of-witchcraft-woman-stripped-killed-in-public/#sthash.5dnKiwl8.dpuf

Oct 22, 2014, BANGALORE: Teacher rapes girl, 4, at Bangalore school
http://m.timesofindia.com/city/bangalore/Teacher-rapes-girl-4-in-Bangalore-school/articleshow/44904069.cms?utm_source=facebook.com&utm_medium=referral&utm_campaign=TOI

October 22, 2014, Ranchi: Woman paraded naked for not bringing dowry
http://www.hindustantimes.com/india-news/ranchi/woman-paraded-naked-filmed-for-not-bringing-dowry/article1-1278192.aspx

October 17, 2014, U.K.: Shunned, beaten, burnt, raped: The dowry violence that shames Britain.
http://www.independent.co.uk/news/uk/crime/shunned-beaten-burnt-raped-the-dowry-violence-that-shames-britain-9803009.html

Oct 15, 2014, Agra: Dentist commits suicide over dowry harassment.
http://m.timesofindia.com/city/agra/Dentist-commits-suicide-over-dowry-harassment/articleshow/44828540.cms

Oct 13, 2014, HYDERABAD: Jilted lover attacks girl with sickle, commits suicide
http://m.timesofindia.com/City/Hyderabad/Jilted-lover-attacks-girl-with-sickle-commits-suicide/articleshow/44800955.cms

Oct 13 2014, HYDRABAD: India's prostitute brides: Girls raped as temporary wives
http://www.thestar.com/news/world/2014/10/13/indias_prostitute_brides_girls_raped_as_temporary_wives.html

Oct 13, 2014, BAREILLY: Teen girl raped, set afire by youth
http://m.timesofindia.com/city/bareilly/Teen-girl-raped-set-afire-by-youth/articleshow/44805303.cms

Oct 12, 2014, BHOPAL: Infant tossed out of moving car, survives
http://m.timesofindia.com/india/Infant-tossed-out-of-moving-car-survives/articleshow/44787920.cms

October 10, 2014, Patna: Five Women Gang-raped at Gun-point in Bihar
http://www.newindianexpress.com/nation/Five-Women-Gang-raped-at-Gun-point-in-Bihar/2014/10/10/article2471023.ece?utm_content=buffer4a557&utm_medium=social&utm_source=twitter.com&utm_campaign=buffer

October 06, 2014, Shillong: Beheaded body of a girl found in Meghalaya
http://www.hindustantimes.com/india-news/beheaded-body-of-a-girl-found-in-meghalaya/article1-1272131.aspx

Oct 4, 2014, Bareilly: Woman dies after being forced to eat cow dung, drink kerosene
http://m.timesofindia.com/city/bareilly/Woman-dies-after-being-forced-to-eat-cow-dung-drink-

kerosene/articleshow/44341330.cms

Oct 4, 2014, Jaipur: Six-year-old girl brutally stabbed to death
http://www.dnaindia.com/india/report-jaipur-six-year-old-girl-brutally-stabbed-to-death-2023527

Oct 3, 2014, Bareilly: Girl found dead on Kanya Puja day
http://m.timesofindia.com/City/Bareilly/Girl-found-dead-on-Kanya-Puja-day/articleshow/44239525.cms

Oct 3, 2014, Patna: Minor girl burnt alive for resisting rape
http://m.timesofindia.com/city/patna/Minor-girl-burnt-alive-for-resisting-rape/articleshow/44220704.cms

Oct 3, 2014, PATNA: Minor girl burnt alive for resisting rape
http://m.timesofindia.com/city/patna/Minor-girl-burnt-alive-for-resisting-rape/articleshow/44220704.cms

Oct 2, 2014, Itanagar: Rape & murder shock Tawang
http://m.timesofindia.com/city/guwahati/Rape–murder-shock-Tawang/articleshow/44019646.cms

Sep 14, 2014, ALLAHABAD: Teenager raped, poisoned to death in UP
http://m.timesofindia.com/City/Allahabad/Teenager-raped-poisoned-to-death-in-UP/articleshow/42437971.cms

Sep 10, 2014, New Delhi: Nirbhaya's nurse alleges gangrape in Punjab, two accused arrested
http://indiatoday.intoday.in/story/nirbhaya-case-nurse-gangraped-punjab-budhlada/1/381943.html

Sep 8, 2014, Darbhanga: Woman Locked Up in Bathroom for Three Years Over Dowry Demand
http://www.ndtv.com/article/cities/woman-locked-up-in-bathroom-for-three-years-over-dowry-demand-588745?site=classic

Sep 6, 2014, India: Consider Husband as Son Under Sharia, Clerics Tell Woman Raped by Father-in-Law
http://www.ibtimes.co.uk/muslim-clerics-india-ask-rape-victim-consider-husband-son-after-she-impregnated-by-father-law-1464310

Sep 6, 2014, Karimganj:Two Schoolgirls Hung From Same Rope on Tree in Assam; Post-mortem Report Expected Today
http://www.ndtv.com/article/india/two-schoolgirls-hung-from-same-rope-on-tree-in-assam-post-mortem-report-expected-today-587590?site=classic

Sep 5, 2014, India: 'House of horrors' cannibal murderer who raped and dismembered 19 young women and children to be hanged in India
http://www.independent.co.uk/news/world/asia/house-of-horrors-cannibal-murderer-who-raped-and-dismembered-19-young-women-and-children-to-be-hanged-in-india-9713807.html

Sep 4, 2014, Bangalore: Dowry Deaths on the Rise
http://www.newindianexpress.com/cities/bangalore/Dowry-Deaths-on-the-Rise/2014/09/04/article2414067.ece

Sep 4, 2014, Bhopal: Man pours acid onto wife's genitals for dowry in Madhya Pradesh
http://m.timesofindia.com/city/bhopal/Man-pours-acid-onto-wifes-genitals-for-dowry-in-Madhya-Pradesh/articleshow/41681419.cms

Sep 3, 2014, Kolkata: Jadavpur University student molested inside boys hostel
http://indiatoday.intoday.in/story/jadavpur-university-student-molested-inside-boys-
hostel/1/380585.html

Sep 3, 2014, Jalpaiguri: She Defied Kangaroo Court's (allegedly led by a woman councilor of
the ruling Trinamool Congress) Order to Lick Spit, Her Naked Body Found Day After
http://www.ndtv.com/article/india/she-defied-kangaroo-court-s-order-to-lick-spit-her-naked-
body-found-day-after-585952?site=classic

Sep 2, 2014, Bareilly: In-laws, hubby kill pregnant woman for dowry
http://m.timesofindia.com/City/Bareilly/In-laws-hubby-kill-pregnant-woman-for-
dowry/articleshow/41542562.cms

Sep 1, 2014, Mumbai: INDIA SHAMED AGAIN: 5-yr-old raped and murdered in Mumbai
http://mdaily.bhaskar.com/news/top-news/4444/NAT-TOP-india-shamed-again-5-yr-old-
raped-and-murdered-in-mumbai-4730826-NOR.html?referrer_url=

Aug 31, 2014, ITANAGAR: Woman raped, murdered while working in her farm in Arunachal
village
http://www.assamtribune.com/scripts/detailsnew.asp?id=sep0114/oth057

Aug 29, 2014, Shantiniketan: Visva Bharati probes sexual assault, women's panel seeks Modi
intervention
http://timesofindia.indiatimes.com/india/3-students-of-Visva-Bharati-expelled-for-stripping-
molesting-a-junior-
student/articleshow/41232071.cms; http://indiatoday.intoday.in/story/vishwa-bharati-probes-
sexual-assault-womens-panel-seeks-modi-
intervention/1/379847.html; http://www.theguardian.com/commentisfree/2010/jun/03/rapes-
india-north-east-prejudice

Aug 27, 2014, Hydrabad: 4 auto drivers held for raping married woman
http://m.timesofindia.com/city/hyderabad/4-auto-drivers-held-for-raping-married-
woman/articleshow/41023055.cms

Aug 20, 2014, Kanpur: Four-year-old girl raped by father's acquaintance in Kanpur
http://zeenews.india.com/news/uttar-pradesh/four-year-old-girl-raped-by-father-s-
acquaintance-in-kanpur_955860.html

Aug 20, 2014, New Delhi: Potency test of accused necessary in rape case: SC
http://zeenews.india.com/news/nation/potency-test-of-accused-necessary-in-rape-case-
sc_955943.html

Aug 19, 2014, Faridabad: Married woman alleges rape by Haryana policeman
http://zeenews.india.com/news/haryana/married-woman-alleges-rape-by-haryana-
policeman_955613.html

Aug 19, 2014, Mumbai: Mumbai cops make molestation victim run from one police station to
another
http://zeenews.india.com/news/maharashtra/mumbai-cops-make-molestation-victim-run-from-
one-police-station-to-another_955501.html

Aug 19, 2014, Muzaffarnagar: Three inmates booked for sodomising 16-year-old inmate
http://zeenews.india.com/news/uttar-pradesh/three-inmates-booked-for-sodomising-16-year-
old-inmate_955533.html

Aug 18, 2014, Jaipur: An 18-year-old girl was allegedly raped here by a youth for three years
on pretext of marriage
http://zeenews.india.com/news/rajasthan/girl-raped-for-three-years-on-pretext-of-marriage-in-
rajasthan_955286.html

Aug 18, 2014, India: Couple's Murder in MP Turns Out to be Honour Killing
http://m.outlookindia.com/news/article/Couples-Murder-in-MP-Turns-Out-to-be-Honour-Killing/855875/

Aug 17, 2014, Delhi: Two minor girls were allegedly raped by their neighbours in two separate cases in the national capital, police said on Sunday
http://zeenews.india.com/news/delhi/two-minors-raped-in-separate-cases-in-delhi_955163.html

Aug 16, 2014, Jaipur: A 16-year-old girl was allegedly gang-raped here by two men who also made a video of the act and used it to blackmail the victim for assaulting her repeatedly http://zeenews.india.com/news/rajasthan/two-youths-rape-16-yr-old-film-the-act-to-blackmail-her_954859.html

Aug 13, 2014, Delhi: year-old girl was allegedly raped by her neighbour when she was sleeping at her home`s terrace in south Delhi Tuesday night
http://zeenews.india.com/news/delhi/minor-raped-while-sleeping-on-terrace-of-house-in-delhi_954425.html

Aug 13, 2014, West Bengal: Relief for Trinamool Congress MP Tapas Pal, a stay has been ordered on registration of FIR and CID probe into his objectionable `rape and shoot` comments against women http://zeenews.india.com/news/west-bengal/relief-for-tmc-mp-tapas-pal-as-hc-stays-filing-of-fir-cid-probe_954224.html

Aug 12, 2014, Delhi: Driver freed of charge of raping maid in employer`s absencehttp://zeenews.india.com/news/delhi/driver-freed-of-charge-of-raping-maid-in-employer-s-absence_953911.html

Aug 12, 2014, Gujarat: Self-styled godman Asaram Bapu`s son Narayan Sai, currently lodged at Surat jail on the charges of rape and conspiring to bribe officials to weaken the case against him http://zeenews.india.com/news/gujarat/hc-issues-notice-to-gujarat-govt-over-narayan-sai-s-bail-petition_953908.html

Aug 11, 2014, DIBRUGARH: In Assam, college students gang-rape teenager
http://m.timesofindia.com/india/In-Assam-college-students-gang-rape-teenager/articleshow/40023469.cms

Aug 5, 2014, New Delhi: Girl jumped off bus to flee molesters
http://timesofindia.indiatimes.com/city/delhi/Girl-jumped-off-bus-to-flee-molesters-Sister/articleshow/39639723.cms

Aug 04, 2014, New Delhi: Alleging Sexual Harassment By High Court Judge, a Junior Female Judge Quits
http://www.ndtv.com/article/india/alleging-sexual-harassment-by-high-court-judge-a-junior-judge-quits-570298?curl=1407316137 ; http://timesofindia.indiatimes.com/india/Sexually-harassed-by-HC-judge-Gwalior-additional-judge-resigns/articleshow/39569700.cms

Aug 04, 2014, Mumbai: Kerala cops face probe by Mumbai Police for abetting rape (Three Kerala Policemen Accused of Organising the Rape of A Woman in Police Custody) http://timesofindia.indiatimes.com/City/Mumbai/Kerala-cops-face-probe-by-Mumbai-Police-for-abetting-rape/articleshow/39568623.cms

Jul 24, 2014, India: Woman asked to hold hot iron rods to prove her chastity.
http://news.oneindia.in/india/dowry-woman-chastity-test-iron-rod-panchayat-madhya-pradesh-1488833.html

Jul 23, 2014, Hyderabad: Tollywood actress Rambha and her brother booked for abuse of sister-in-law.

http://www.deccanchronicle.com/140723/nation-crime/article/actor-rambha-and-her-brother-booked-abuse-sister-law

Jul 23, 2014, Mathura: Six held in Mathura rape case.
http://www.deccanchronicle.com/140723/nation-crime/article/six-held-mathura-rape-case

Jul 23, 2014, Muzaffarnagar: Woman abducted and gang-raped.
http://www.hindustantimes.com/india-news/woman-abducted-and-gangraped-in-muzaffarnagar/article1-1243616.aspx

Jul 21, 2014, Aizawl: Mizoram Woman gang-raped in front of her husband.
http://www.hindustantimes.com/india-news/woman-gangraped-in-front-of-husband/article1-1242871.aspx

Jul 18-19, 2014, Bangalore: 6 year old minor girl raped in school.
http://m.timesofindia.com/city/bangalore/Sexual-assault-on-girl-came-to-light-after-stranger-called-mother/articleshow/38572435.cms ;
http://timesofindia.indiatimes.com/Entertainment/Events/Bangalore/Bangalore-parents-protest-against-minors-rape-in-school/articleshow/38667212.cms ; http://timesofindia.indiatimes.com/city/bangalore/Thousan ds-protest-6-year-olds-rape-in-Bangalore-school-want-suspects-arrested/articleshow/38688058.cms ; http://www.ndtv.com/article/south/bangalore-school-rape-it-happened-to-my-daughter-too-561465

Jul 19, 2014, Lucknow: Woman's naked body had been found lying in a pool of blood.
http://www.hindustantimes.com/india-news/lucknow-rape-murder-cops-detain-key-accused/article1-1242435.aspx ; http://www.hindustantimes.com/india-news/lucknow/lucknow-rape-murder-cops-say-close-to-cracking-case-as-cm-asks-to-intensify-probe/article1-1242239.aspx

Jul 18, 2014, Badhohi, Uttar Pradesh: Wife of a Government employee, gang raped by lawyer and constable.
http://zeenews.india.com/news/uttar-pradesh/woman-raped-by-lawyer-constable-in-up_948266.html

Jul 11, 2014, Jharkhand: 10 year old raped on village head's order to seek revenge.
http://www.deccanchronicle.com/140711/nation-crime/article/jharkhand-10-year-old-raped-village-heads-order-seek-revenge

Jul 9, 2014, New Delhi: 81 year old journalist raped, strangled, and set on fire in her South Delhi Home.
http://www.ndtv.com/article/india/81-year-old-allegedly-raped-strangled-set-on-fire-by-help-in-south-delhi-home-555659 ; http://timesofindia.indiatimes.com/City/Delhi/Journalists-81-year-old-widow-was-raped-before-murder/articleshow/38093624.cms

Jul 7, 2014, Mumbai: Security guard who killed advocate Pallavi on 10th Aug 2012, is sentenced to life.
http://ibnlive.in.com/news/security-guard-who-killed-pallavi-purkayastha-sentenced-to-life/484264-3-237.html

Jul 6, 2014, New Delhi: Incest rape on the rise.
http://timesofindia.indiatimes.com/india/Incest-rape-on-the-rise-according-to-NCRB-data/articleshow/37876712.cms

Jul 2, 2014, West Bengal: Sexual Assault on child in kindergarten.
http://timesofindia.indiatimes.com/city/kolkata/Sexual-assault-on-child-in-kindergarten/articleshow/37613141.cms ; http://violenceonindianwomen.wordpress.com/2014/07/28/a-3-year-old-kindergarten-girl-sexually-assaulted-in-school-in-west-bengal/

Jul 1, 2014, Kolkata: Caught on camera, TMC MP Tapas Pal openly threatens rape, murder.
http://zeenews.india.com/news/west-bengal/caught-on-camera-tmc-mp-tapas-pal-openly-threatens-rape-murder_944022.html
http://violenceonindianwomen.wordpress.com/2014/07/02/member-of-indias-parliament-threatens-to-send-his-boys-to-rape-women/

June 29, 2014, West Bengal: Another woman pushed off train.
http://timesofindia.indiatimes.com/city/kolkata/Another-woman-pushed-off-train-in-Bengal/articleshow/37423818.cms

June 28, 2014, Lucknow: Minors raped and killed.
http://indianexpress.com/article/cities/lucknow/minors-raped-killed-in-bahraich-amethi/

June 26, 2014, Washington: US negotiating MoU with India on women's issues.
http://zeenews.india.com/news/nation/us-negotiating-mou-with-india-on-women-s-issues_942834.html

June 25, 2014, New Delhi: "Don't wear condom, wear values to fight AIDS": Dr. Harsh Vardhan, Indian Health Minister.
http://economictimes.indiatimes.com/news/politics-and-nation/dont-wear-a-condom-wear-values-to-fight-aids-dr-harsh-vardhan-health-minister/articleshow/37146142.cms ; http://timesofindia.indiatimes.com/India/Health-minister-Dr-Harsh-Vardhan-questions-stress-on-condoms-in-AIDS-fight/articleshow/37173742.cms

June 25, 2014, Jaipur: Transgender raped by a police in Ajmer.
http://www.thehindu.com/news/national/transgender-raped-by-police-in-ajmer/article6146114.ece?homepage=true

June 25, 2014, Muzaffarnagar: Girl gang-raped by eight youths, video uploaded on Facebook. http://zeenews.india.com/news/uttar-pradesh/muzaffarnagar-girl-gang-raped-by-eight-youths-video-uploaded-on-facebook_942532.html

June 24, 2014, Mumbai: Actress Preity Zinta reaches Wankhede to record statement against ex, for rape threats and harrasements.
http://www.hindustantimes.com/entertainment/tabloid/preity-zinta-reaches-wankhede-stadium-to-record-her-statement/article1-1233176.aspx?hts0021

June 24, 2014, Thane: Woman from Thane taken to MP, 'raped' and then forced into flesh trade.
http://zeenews.india.com/news/maharashtra/thane-woman-taken-to-mp-andquot-rapedandquot-and-forced-into-flesh-trade_942219.html

June 23, 2014, Rajasthan: Village council convened abused woman's family to pay Rs.2 lakhs (U.S.$4000/-) to the in-laws, ostracised for filing a law suit against their in-laws. http://www.hindustantimes.com/india-news/jaipur/woman-s-family-fined-rs-2-lakh-ostracised-for-filing-dowry-case/article1-1230400.aspx

June 23, 2014, Muzzafarnagar, Uttar Pradesh: 7Years old Gang Raped by Three Men. http://www.deccanchronicle.com/140623/nation-crime/article/uttar-pradesh-shocker-7-year-old-girl-gangraped-muzaffarnagar

June 22, 2014, New Delhi: Woman gang raped in parking of a five star hotel in Delhi. http://zeenews.india.com/news/delhi/woman-gang-raped-in-parking-of-five-star-hotel-in-delhi_941405.html

June 21, 2014, Kanpur: Woman sets herself ablaze with twins.
http://timesofindia.indiatimes.com/city/kanpur/Woman-sets-self-ablaze-with-twins/articleshow/36945065.cms

June 20, 2014, Delhi: American studying sex assault in India recounts her own attack. http://america.aljazeera.com/articles/2014/6/20/india-sex-assaultstudent.html

June 18, 2014, Ahmadabad, Gujarat: 16-year-old Dalit girl was doused with kerosene and set on fire by her neighbours at Sayla village in Surendranagar district of Gujarat. http://www.ndtv.com/article/india/girl-allegedly-set-on-fire-after-fight-over-sewage-line-in-gujarat-543419

June 17, 2014, India: Better toilets won't solve India's rape problem. http://america.aljazeera.com/opinions/2014/6/better-toilets-wontsolveindiasrapeproblem.html

June 15, 2014, Agra, UP: Family attempts honour killing of 16-yr-old girl impregnated by rape. http://timesofindia.indiatimes.com/city/lucknow/Pregnant-rape-survivor-tied-up-dumped-in-river-by-mom-uncle/articleshow/36575709.cms

June 16, 2014, India: Indian State minister vows action on rapes. http://www.sbs.com.au/news/article/2014/06/16/indian-state-minister-vows-action-rapes

June 16, 2014, Khandwa, Madhya Pradesh: Tribal woman was paraded naked, then gang raped by her husband and 9 other men. http://indianexpress.com/article/india/india-others/tribal-woman-gangraped-by-10-persons-including-husband-paraded-naked/

June 15, 2014, India: Rape in India: Reading between the lines. http://america.aljazeera.com/articles/2014/6/15/rape-in-india-readingbetweenthelines.html

June 14, 2014, Bangalore: MNC Executive Tries to Kill Wife for Dowry By Force Feeding Her Toilet Cleaner. http://timesofindia.indiatimes.com/city/bangalore/Man-forces-wife-to-drink-toilet-cleaner-over-dowry/articleshow/36511193.cms

June 12, 2014, India: Indian police investigate alleged station gang rape. http://america.aljazeera.com/articles/2014/6/12/india-woman-gangrape.html

June 12, 2014, Bhadohi: Woman killed by doctor husband over dowry. http://www.business-standard.com/article/pti-stories/woman-killed-by-doctor-husband-over-dowry-114061201043_1.html

June 9, 2014, India: India's caste culture is a Rape Culture. http://www.thedailybeast.com/witw/articles/2014/06/09/india-s-caste-culture-is-a-rape-culture.html

June 8, 2014, Tripura: Mentally Challenged Woman Gang Raped, Killed and Burnt in Tripura. http://www.northeasttoday.in/news.php?news=woman-gangraped,-burnt-to-death-in-tripura-

June 8, 2014, Jaipur, Rajasthan: Female corporate official of a Malaysian company was drugged and raped by a man at gunpoint http://www.asianage.com/india/malaysia-woman-raped-gunpoint-039

June 6, 2014, Hyderabad: 24-year-old housewife burnt to death by her husband and in-laws, for dowry. http://timesofindia.indiatimes.com/city/hyderabad/Woman-burnt-alive-for-dowry-in-Hyderabad/articleshow/36112359.cms

June 6, 2014, India: Indian politician claims 'rape:sometimes right, sometimes wrong'. http://www.nzherald.co.nz/world/news/article.cfm?c_id=2&objectid=11268684; http://www.nydailynews.com/news/world/indian-politician-claims-rape-article-1.1819496; http://www.sbs.com.au/news/article/2014/06/06/rape-sometimes-right-indian-minister

June 5, 2014, Meghalaya: Woman shot point blank, six times in the head for resisting gang rape. http://www.ndtv.com/article/india/meghalaya-encounter-on-with-militants-who-killed-woman-in-front-of-her-children-536242

June 3, 2014, Meerut: In U.P., 10-year-old gang-rape survivor abducted. http://timesofindia.indiatimes.com/india/In-UP-10-year-old-gang-rape-survivor-abducted/articleshow/35976045.cms

June 3, 2014, Aligarh, Uttar Pradesh: Gang rape and attempted murder of a Woman Judge in Uttar Pradesh. http://indiatoday.intoday.in/story/rape-in-uttara-pradesh-a-woman-judge-raped/1/365058.html

June 2, 2014, Bareilly, Uttar Pradesh: Gang rape victim's face burnt with acid, and forced to drink acid. http://timesofindia.indiatimes.com/city/hyderabad/Woman-burnt-alive-for-dowry-in-Hyderabad/articleshow/36112359.cms ; http://www.dailymail.co.uk/news/article-2646225/Indian-police-fire-water-cannon-anti-rape-protesters.html

May 31, 2014, Jalgaon, Maharashtra: Woman dies after being 'pushed' off train at Jalgaon. http://www.thehindu.com/news/national/other-states/woman-dies-after-being-pushed-off-train-at-jalgoan/article6061553.ece

May 30, 2014, Badaun: India gang rapes: Outrage over police 'discrimination'. http://www.bbc.com/news/world-asia-india-27631241

May 30, 2014, Mumbai: Systematic rape and Sexual Torture of Children in a shelter near Mumbai. http://news.oneindia.in/mumbai/children-raped-forced-to-eat-excreta-in-maharashtra-shelter-1456793.html ; http://violenceonindianwomen.wordpress.com/2012/06/07/minor-girls-in-indian-orphanage-raped-by-police/ ; http://www.outlookindia.com/news/article/Children-Raped-Forced-to-Eat-Excreta-at-Shelter-Home/842349 ; http://wcd.nic.in/childabuse.pdf

May 30, 2014, Palakkad: Nearly 600 trafficked kids rescued from Kerala. http://indiatoday.intoday.in/story/600-trafficked-kids-rescued-from-kerala/1/364115.html

May 29-30, 2014, Badayun, Uttar Pradesh (U.P.): Two teenage girls were gang raped by 5 men, including two police constables, and then hanged to death. http://economictimes.indiatimes.com/news/politics-and-nation/two-minor-dalit-girls-raped-and-hanged-in-uttar-pradesh/articleshow/35741642.cms ; http://zeenews.india.com/news/uttar-pradesh/two-dalit-sisters-gang-raped-hanged-from-tree-in-up-4-arrested_935769.html ; http://timesofindia.indiatimes.com/topic/Minor-Girl's-Gang-Rape-and-Murder

May 26, 2014, New Delhi: 6 rapes daily in Delhi, says police data. http://www.hindustantimes.com/india-news/newdelhi/six-rapes-daily-in-capital-city-says-police-data/article1-1222882.aspx

May 16, 2014, Kanpur: Man sets wife ablaze, infant for more dowries. http://timesofindia.indiatimes.com/city/kanpur/Man-sets-ablaze-wife-infant-for-more-dowry/articleshow/35176832.cms

14 May 2014, New Delhi: Girl kills self after boyfriend refuses to marry her over dowry. http://www.dnaindia.com/india/report-delhi-girl-kills-self-after-boyfriend-refuses-to-marry-her-over-dowry-1988385

May 12, 2014, Bareilly: BSP leader aids booked for 'raping' Dalit. http://timesofindia.indiatimes.com/india/BSP-leader-aides-booked-for-raping-dalit/articleshow/34993111.cms

May 11, 2014, Indore: Classmates rape girl, burn her to
death. http://timesofindia.indiatimes.com/City/Indore/23-year-old-pharmacy-girl-dies-after-
rape-set-ablaze-by-college-mates/articleshow/34980689.cms

May 11, 2014, Dibrugarh, Assam: Attempted murder of a medical intern on duty in hospital in
Assam. http://indianexpress.com/article/india/india-others/in-assam-hospital-ward-boy-kills-
medical-student-inside-icu/ ; Similar case in
1973: http://en.wikipedia.org/wiki/Aruna_Shanbaug_case

May 11, 2014, Lucknow: AMU professor suspended for molesting foreign
student. http://indiatoday.intoday.in/story/aligarh-muslim-university-professor-suspended-
molesting-foreign-student/1/360144.html

May 1, 2014, Nagpur, Maharashtra: Dowry torture: Woman ends life with 9-year-old
daughter. http://timesofindia.indiatimes.com/city/nagpur/Dowry-torture-Woman-ends-life-with-
9-year-old-daughter/articleshow/34441525.cms

April 27, 2014, Nagpur: Holy Godman rapes 17-year-old girl promising
miracle. http://timesofindia.indiatimes.com/city/nagpur/Godman-rapes-17-year-old-girl-
promising-miracle/articleshow/34268288.cms

April 25, 2014, Bundi, Rajasthan: Teacher gang-raped in school premises in
Rajasthan. http://timesofindia.indiatimes.com/city/jaipur/Teacher-gang-raped-in-school-
premises-in-Rajasthan/articleshow/34209882.cms

April 20, 2014, New Delhi: The death of 254 Indian women from modest backgrounds in the
course of a 15-year US-funded clinical trial. http://timesofindia.indiatimes.com/india/Row-over-
clinical-trial-as-254-Indian-women-
die/articleshow/34016785.cms ; http://www.nature.com/news/2011/110622/full/474427a.html ;
 http://www.australasianscience.com.au/article/issue-october-2013/care-and-consent-fraught-
ethics-international-clinical-trials.html ; http://www.bihardays.com/making-living-guinea-pig-
india-clinical-trials-drug-companies/

Apr 24, 2014, Hazaribagh, Jharkhand: Jharkhand woman gives kidney to husband as dowry,
kills self after six months.
http://timesofindia.indiatimes.com/city/ranchi/Jharkhand-woman-gives-kidney-to-husband-as-
dowry-kills-self-after-six-months/articleshow/34135681.cms

April 18, 2014, Bangalore: Irish tourist was sexually assaulted waiting for her train in the
station's waiting room at 6am. http://www.mid-day.com/articles/irish-tourist-molested-at-
bangalore-railway-station/15239052

April 9, 2014, Muzzafarnagar, Uttar Pradesh: Husband and in-laws, for dowry, allegedly
strangulated woman to death.
http://www.abplive.in/crime/2014/04/09/article291733.ece/Woman-killed-over-dowry-by-
husband-and-in-laws#.U6ixvijiw05

April 5, 2014, Annamalai, Tamil Nadu: 50-year-old woman strangulated to
death. http://www.business-standard.com/article/pti-stories/50-year-old-woman-strangulated-
to-death-114040900728_1.html

April 05, 2014, Agra, Uttar Pradesh: 14-year-old schoolgirl raped in
Agra. http://timesofindia.indiatimes.com/India/14-year-old-schoolgirl-raped-in-
Agra/articleshow/33273118.cms

April 09, 2014, Thane: Thane: Two minor girls allegedly
raped. http://www.ndtv.com/article/cities/thane-two-minor-girls-allegedly-raped-506249

April 09, 2014, Pune, Maharashtra: Unemployed man kills mother, wife, daughter;
surrenders. http://www.business-standard.com/article/pti-stories/unemployed-man-kills-
mother-wife-daughter-surrenders-114040901431_1.html

April 8, 2014, Pune, Maharashtra: Two held for raping 15-year-old in
Warje. http://timesofindia.indiatimes.com/city/pune/Two-held-for-raping-15-year-old-in-
Warje/articleshow/33409196.cms

April 7, 2014, Agra: Agra hotel manager tries to rape German
tourist. http://indiatoday.intoday.in/story/agra-hotel-manager-tries-to-rape-german-
tourist/1/353447.html

April 04, 2014, Srinagar, Jammu and Kashmir: newborn baby girl, was discovered drowned in
a bucket of water in a public bathroom in Kashmir. http://kashmirpioneer.com/news/3875-
kashmir-newborn-girl-killed-by-immersing-her-in-a-bucket-of-water-at-
rainawari ; http://timesofindia.indiatimes.com/india/JK-sees-biggest-decline-in-child-sex-ratio-
in-country/articleshow/8053244.cms

April 3, 2014, Thane, Maharashtra: Five booked for kicking pregnant housewife over dowry
demands. http://www.deccanherald.com/content/396455/five-booked-kicking-pregnant-
housewife.html

March 30, 2014, Rajahmundry: Pregnant woman burnt alive for dowry in
Andhra. http://www.hindustantimes.com/india-news/pregnant-woman-burnt-alive-for-dowry-in-
andhra/article1-1202167.aspx

March 30, 2014, Delhi: Woman gang-raped by doctor, aid in south Delhi's Hauz Khas
area. http://www.dnaindia.com/india/report-woman-gang-raped-by-doctor-aide-in-south-delhi-
s-hauz-khas-area-1973697

March 30, 2014: Women politicians face sexist slurs, pawing; seek safety inside
cars. http://timesofindia.indiatimes.com/news/Women-politicians-face-sexist-slurs-pawing-
seek-safety-inside-cars/articleshow/32934688.cms?

March 29, 2014, Mirzapur, U.P.: Female journalist gang raped
in UP. http://indianexpress.com/article/india/india-others/ukhand-scribe-gangraped-in-up/

March 24, 2014, Kolkata: Actor and Trinamool candidate Dev Adhikari says Rape is to be
enjoyed.
http://www.firstpost.com/election-diary/bengali-actor-politicians-enjoy-rape-remark-the-
medias-an-equal-sinner-1447737.html
http://ibnlive.in.com/news/bengali-star-trinamool-candidate-dev-reminds-us-why-rape-jokes-
are-always-inappropriate-and-why-we-wont-lighten-up/460019-37-64.html
http://www.newindianexpress.com/nation/Actor-Dev-Says-Joining-Election-Fray-Is-Like-
Getting-Raped/2014/03/24/article2128170.ece

March 24, 2014, Hyderabad: Indian female engineer murdered by her for marrying the man
she loved: parents in suspected honour killing.
http://timesofindia.indiatimes.com/city/hyderabad/Techie-murdered-by-parents-in-suspected-
honour-killing/articleshow/32575093.cms

March 23, 2014, Thane, Maharashtra: Woman resists sex work, pimps cut off her
breasts. http://www.hindustantimes.com/india-news/breasts-chopped-off-for-refusing-to-enter-
flesh-trade/article1-1199182.aspx

Mar 19, 2014, Dehradun, India: 16-year-old girl raped and forced into abortion in India, police say.
http://www.lifesitenews.com/news/16-year-old-girl-raped-and-forced-into-abortion-in-india-police-say

March 18, 2014, Unnao (UP): Honour killing of al couple.
http://www.thehindu.com/news/national/other-states/honour-killing-father-murders-daughter-soninlaw/article5800420.ece

March 15, 2014, India: Persecution of Indian Women: Documentary Exposes Abortion, Sex Trafficking, Rape. http://www.christianpost.com/news/persecution-of-indian-women-documentary-exposes-abortion-sex-trafficking-rape-116164/

March 14, 2014, Cuttack, Orissa: 2008 Kandhamal nun gang rape case: 3 convicted, 6 acquitted.
http://indiatoday.intoday.in/story/2008-kandhamal-nun-gangrape-3-convicted-6-acquitted/1/349507.html ; http://www.hindu.com/2008/09/30/stories/2008093058040100.htm

March 10, 2014, Women feel gender based violence is widespread.
http://www.business-standard.com/article/pti-stories/women-feel-gender-based-violence-is-widespread-114031000520_1.html

March 7, 2014, Delhi: Judge Says Sunita's is not a Dowry Murder Because Her Marriage May be Illegal? http://www.business-standard.com/article/pti-stories/can-t-be-held-for-dowry-harassment-if-marriage-is-doubtful-114030700847_1.html ; Sunita's Case file here http://indiankanoon.org/doc/1527429/ ; http://genderbytes.wordpress.com/2011/10/02/video-murder-by-fire-100000-women-a-year/ – Rita Banerji's 50Million Missing Campaign : http://genderbytes.wordpress.com/2010/11/22/dowry-laws-every-indian-must-know/ – Dowry Laws

March 05, 2014, Raipur, Chhattisgarh: Woman branded witch, mercilessly killed in Chhattisgarh. http://timesofindia.indiatimes.com/city/raipur/Woman-branded-witch-mercilessly-killed-in-Chhattisgarh/articleshow/31486503.cms ; http://fridaymagazine.ae/features/the-big-story/the-witch-hunts-of-india-1.1227329

Feb 10-11, 2014 Chennai: After 17-year battle, Captain Latha to be reinstated in Army. http://articles.timesofindia.indiatimes.com/2014-02-10/chennai/47199906_1_army-staff-armed-forces-tribunal-high-court ; http://www.ibtimes.com/kunan-poshpora-can-kashmiri-rape-victims-get-justice-against-indian-military-after-two-decades ; http://www.newindianexpress.com/opinion/pointofview/Armys-right-to-rape-and-kill-must-go-if-Northeast-is-to-be-part-of-India/2013/04/14/article1543771.ece

Feb 9, 2014, Howrah, West Bengal: Two women who families voted for the CPI (M) or communist party were gang raped by 7 men from the opposition, ruling party. http://ibnlive.in.com/news/howrah-gangrape-case-prime-accused-arrested/450824-3-231.html

Feb 02, 2014, Jharkhand: Indian wife and her baby daughter burned to death by husband as the mother breastfed her little girl because he wanted a son. http://www.dailymail.co.uk/news/article-2549975/Young-Indian-mother-baby-daughter-burned-death-failing-pay-new-family-dowry.html#ixzz2sWe0uayH

Feb 02, 2014, Manipur: Racist assault of two Manipuri women in Delhi. http://genderbytes.wordpress.com/2011/09/26/unknown-faces-of-indian-women-an-online-photo-exhibition/ ; http://ibnlive.in.com/news/delhi-manipur-women-assaulted-beaten-by-men-1-arrested/449513-3-244.html ; http://indiatoday.intoday.in/story/nido-taniam-murder-delhis-racism-caused-arunachal-students-death-cries-northeast/1/341045.html

Jan 31, 2014, Mumbai: Mumbai crime: Gas delivery men rape woman, loot cash, jewellery –
http://www.mid-day.com/articles/mumbai-crime-gas-delivery-men-rape-woman-loot-cash-
jewellery/15060044#sthash.Yx9XPgYu.dpuf

Jan 30, 2014, Bareilly: Honour killing of teenage girl shocks
Bareilly. http://timesofindia.indiatimes.com/city/lucknow/Honour-killing-of-teenage-girl-shocks-
Bareilly/articleshow/29581676.cms

Jan 25, 2014, Mumbai: Mumbai dance teacher raped by building
guard. http://indiatoday.intoday.in/story/mumbai-dance-teacher-powai-raped-by-building-
guard/1/339805.html

Jan 22, 2014, (Birbhum district) West Bengal: Tribal woman gang-raped by 10 men following
kangaroo court's diktat.
http://timesofindia.indiatimes.com/city/kolkata/Tribal-woman-gang-raped-by-10-men-following-
kangaroo-courts-diktat/articleshow/29215271.cms ; http://www.ndtv.com/article/india/west-
bengal-woman-allegedly-gang-raped-as-punishment-on-orders-of-kangaroo-court-
474433?curl=1390461965

Jan 21, 2014, Kolkata, West Bengal: 21-year-old girl gang-raped for 2 hours in Kolkata,
battered, bleeding, walks for 3.5kms in search of help.
http://timesofindia.indiatimes.com/city/kolkata/21-year-old-girl-gang-raped-for-2-hours-in-
Kolkata-1-held/articleshow/29127062.cms

Jan 17, 2014, Jaipur, Abandoned, newborn battles for life in chill.
http://timesofindia.indiatimes.com/city/jaipur/Abandoned-newborn-battles-for-life-in-
chill/articleshow/28920566.cms?referral=PM

Jan 17, 2014, Delhi: Danish tourist gang raped in
Delhi. http://www.thehindu.com/news/national/danish-tourist-gangraped-in-
delhi/article5577707.ece

Jan 16, 2014, New Delhi: Former SC judge denies sexual harassment
allegations. http://ibnlive.in.com/news/former-sc-judge-swatanter-kumar-denies-sexual-
assault-allegations/444685-3-244.html

Jan 11, 2014, Chennai: India: Man arrested for allegedly raping a German teen in moving
train. https://hromedia.com/2014/01/15/india-man-arrested-allegedly-raping-a-german-teen-in-
moving-train/

Jan 11, 2014, Kumbakonam, Tamil Nadu: Murdered ruthlessly cause she was born a
female. http://www.business-standard.com/article/pti-stories/newborn-girl-baby-found-
murdered-114011100538_1.html

Jan 11, 2014, Mumbai: Fashion designer pushed into
prostitution. http://timesofindia.indiatimes.com/city/mumbai/Fashion-designer-pushed-into-
prostitution/articleshow/28653361.cms

Jan 09, 2014, Uttarakhand: 13-year old dalit girl was gang-raped and tortured before being
killed in Uttarakhand's Haridwar district.
http://articles.timesofindia.indiatimes.com/2014-01-09/india/46028771_1_dalit-girl-
uttarakhand-chief-minister-haridwar

Jan 5, 2014, Kolkata, West Bengal: Molested woman, kin scared of leaving
home. http://timesofindia.indiatimes.com/city/kolkata/Molested-woman-kin-scared-of-leaving-
home/articleshow/28418657.cms?referral=PM

Jan 04, 2014, Gorakhpur, UP: Woman beaten to death for
dowry. http://timesofindia.indiatimes.com/city/varanasi/Woman-beaten-to-death-for-
dowry/articleshow/28432607.cms?referral=PM

Jan 04, 2014, Ludhiana: NGO adopts baby left in hospital
toilet. http://timesofindia.indiatimes.com/city/ludhiana/NGO-adopts-baby-left-in-hospital-
toilet/articleshow/28375603.cms?referral=PM

Jan 04, 2014, Mumbai: 55-year-old ragpicker woman raped, murdered in
Ghatkopar. http://timesofindia.indiatimes.com/city/mumbai/55-year-old-woman-raped-
murdered-in-Ghatkopar/articleshow/28251991.cms?referral=PM

Jan 03, 2014, Guwahati: 850 dowry deaths in last six
years. http://www.assamtribune.com/scripts/detailsnew.asp?id=jan0414/at085

Jan 03, 2014, Kolkata, West Bengal: Police failed twice to protect Kolkata gang-rape
victim. http://timesofindia.indiatimes.com/city/kolkata/Police-failed-twice-to-protect-Kolkata-
gang-rape-
victim/articleshow/28305814.cms?keepThis=true&TB_iframe=true&height=650&width=850&c
aption=World+-+Google+News ; http://indiatoday.intoday.in/story/kolkata-murdered-gangrape-
victim-was-pregnant-say-west-bengal-
police/1/334003.html ; http://www.dailymail.co.uk/news/article-2532514/Police-hijack-hearse-
try-forcibly-cremate-body-Indian-girl-16-committed-suicide-gang-raped-twice-politically-
protected-mobsters.html ; http://violenceonindianwomen.wordpress.com/2014/01/03/girl-in-
kolkata-gang-raped-twice-and-burnt-to-death-as-police-looked-away/

Dec 31, 2013, Andhra Pradesh: Crimes Against Women on the
Rise. http://violenceonindianwomen.wordpress.com/2014/01/06/crimes-against-women-on-
the-rise-in-andhra-pradesh/

Dec 29, 2013, India: 3 states with the highest rates of crimes against women in
India. http://ibnlive.in.com/news/shame-map-of-india-states-with-highest-rate-of-crimes-
against-women/416615-53.html

Dec 29, 2013, Karnataka: Husband forces wife to drink his urine for more
dowries. http://ibnlive.in.com/news/karnataka-husband-forces-wife-to-drink-his-urine-for-more-
dowry/271264-62-129.html

Dec 24, 2013, Kolkata: 13-year-old girl kidnapped near Park Street, gang-
raped. http://timesofindia.indiatimes.com/city/kolkata/13-year-old-girl-kidnapped-near-Park-
Street-gang-raped/articleshow/27811229.cms?referral=PM

Dec 19, 2013, Tirumangalam: Doc Booked for Demanding Rs 1 Cr Dowry to Set up
Hosp. http://www.newindianexpress.com/states/tamil_nadu/Doc-Booked-for-Demanding-Rs-
1-Cr-Dowry-to-Set-up-Hosp/2013/12/19/article1953248.ece

Dec 19, 2013, Raipur: Labelled 'witch', gang-raped by villagers.
http://www.kractivist.org/dalit-woman-labelled-witch-and-gangraped-in-public-vaw-wtfnews/

Dec 12, 2013, Bangalore: IAF officer arrested for dowry harassment; driving wife to
suicide. http://www.newskarnataka.com/news/content/state/IAF-officer-arrested-for-dowry-
harassment-driving-wife-to-suicide

Dec 6, 2013, Katihar, Bihar: Panchayat orders Bihar girl to marry and pay dowry to her
'rapist'. http://www.hindustantimes.com/india-news/panchayat-orders-bihar-girl-to-marry-and-
pay-dowry-to-her-rapist/article1-1159900.aspx

Dec 6, 2013, Mumbai: Husband sells wife to allow a gang rape on
her. http://timesofindia.indiatimes.com/city/mumbai/Woman-shared-by-hubby-for-Rs-1-5-lakh-
gang-raped/articleshow/26925888.cms

Dec 4, 2013, Time Magazine, World: Top 10 International News Stories, No.9. India's Rape
Epidemic. http://world.time.com/2013/12/04/world/slide/top-10-international-news-stories/

Nov 25, 2013, Assam: Pregnant Woman Hacked to Death for
Dowry. http://zeenews.india.com/news/assam/pregnant-woman-s-body-found-dowry-threat-
suspected-in-assam_892388.html

Nov 27, 2013, Bangalore: Teenager gang raped by her boyfriend and his
friends. http://timesofindia.indiatimes.com/city/bangalore/Teenager-gang-raped-in-
Bangalore/articleshow/26437214.cms

Nov 27, 2013, Mumbai: 17 year old girl gang raped in
Mumbai. http://timesofindia.indiatimes.com/city/mumbai/Minor-gang-raped-on-Borivli-Link-
Road/articleshow/26437581.cms

Nov 26, 2013, 50 Million Missing: Arundhati Roy breaks the liberal conspiracy of scilence
around the Tehelka rape.
http://violenceonindianwomen.wordpress.com/2013/11/26/arundhati-roy-breaks-the-liberal-
conspiracy-of-silence-around-the-tehelka-rape/

Nov 20-26, 2013, Delhi: Prominent Editor and Rights Activists in India
Charged. http://violenceonindianwomen.wordpress.com/2013/11/26/prominent-editor-and-
rights-activist-in-india-charged-with-rape/ ;
http://www.dnaindia.com/india/report-tehelka-editor-tarun-tejpal-charged-with-rape-victim-
resigns-1922519 ;
http://www.thehindu.com/opinion/lead/issues-of-sexual-assault-the-tehelka-
case/article5386951.ece ;
Also see: http://en.wikipedia.org/wiki/Tarun_Tejpal

Nov 15, 2013, Delhi: Ex-DU dean seeks FIR on law intern's sex
charge. http://timesofindia.indiatimes.com/india/Ex-DU-dean-seeks-FIR-on-law-interns-sex-
charge/articleshow/25782569.cms?referral=PM ;
http://www.thehindu.com/todays-paper/tp-national/tp-newdelhi/file-fir-in-intern-case-exdean-
to-police/article5353486.ece ;
http://violenceonindianwomen.wordpress.com/2013/11/17/ex-professor-files-police-complaint-
of-sexual-harassment-of-students-against-supreme-court-judge/

Nov15, 2013, Kanpur: Plaint against CBI chief for rape
remark. http://timesofindia.indiatimes.com/city/kanpur/Plaint-against-CBI-chief-for-rape-
remark/articleshow/25782273.cms?referral=PM

Nov 13, 2013, Delhi: SC yet to form panel to probe sexual harassment
charges. http://timesofindia.indiatimes.com/india/SC-yet-to-form-panel-to-probe-sexual-
harassment-charges/articleshow/25663006.cms?referral=PM

Nov. 08, 2013, Delhi: Time Magazine, Why Rape Seems Worse in India Than Everywhere
Else (but Actually Isn't).
http://world.time.com/2013/11/08/why-rape-seems-worse-in-india-than-everywhere-else-but-
actually-isnt/

Nov 6, 2013, Mumbai: Girl raped, killed by father and friends.
http://indianexpress.com/article/cities/mumbai/girl-raped-killed-by-father-his-friend/

Nov 6, 2013, Indore: Man sets wife on fire for dowry.
http://timesofindia.indiatimes.com/city/indore/Man-sets-wife-on-fire-for-dowry/articleshow/25286021.cms?referral=PM

Nov 4, 2013, Mumbai: Mumbai gang-rape victim asks court for 'permission to slap her attackers'. http://www.dailymail.co.uk/indiahome/indianews/article-2480476/Mumbai-gang-rape-victim-asks-court-permission-slap-attackers.html#ixzz35Y6koW3Y

Nov 3, 2013, Delhi: Ex-Congress MLA arrested in dowry death case. http://m.ibnlive.com/news/india/delhi-excongress-mla-arrested-in-dowry-death-case/432032-3.html

Nov 2, 2013, Kanpur: Woman lynched for dowry by husband in Kanpur Dehat. http://timesofindia.indiatimes.com/city/kanpur/Woman-lynched-for-dowry-by-husband-in-Kanpur-Dehat/articleshow/25092736.cms?referral=PM

Nov 1, 2013, Mumbai: Dowry death: HC upholds life term of hubby, in-laws. http://www.dnaindia.com/mumbai/report-dowry-death-hc-upholds-life-term-of-hubby-in-laws-1912197

Nov 1, 2013, Haryana: For dowry, Haryana man forces wife to have sodomy. http://www.indiatvnews.com/crime/news/for-dowry-haryana-man-forces-wife-to-have-unnatural-sex-4266.html

October 29, 2013, Ahmadabad: Woman continuously raped by her husband with who she is separated. http://timesofindia.indiatimes.com/city/ahmedabad/Woman-accuses-husband-of-rape/articleshow/24876562.cms?referral=PM

October 26, 2013, Mumbai: Gang Rape in India, Routine and Invisible. http://www.nytimes.com/2013/10/27/world/asia/gang-rape-in-india-routine-and-invisible.html?pagewanted=all&_r=0

October 02, 2013, Delhi: 18 years after complaint, 61-year-old woman & son jailed in dowry case. http://www.ndtv.com/article/cities/18-years-after-complaint-61-year-old-woman-son-jailed-in-dowry-case-426781

Sep 6, 2013, Delhi: Has Delhi forgotten the five-year-old girl who was raped? http://ibnlive.in.com/news/has-delhi-forgotten-the-fiveyearold-girl-who-was-raped/419984-3-244.html

Aug 16, 2013, India: Partition of India & Pakistan saw the rape of women at an epic historic scale. http://www.ibtimes.com/partition-india-pakistan-rape-women-epic-historic-scale-1387601

Aug 16, 2013, Delhi: AIIMS nurses victims of wife beating. http://www.thehindu.com/news/cities/Delhi/article3778669.ece ;
http://violenceonindianwomen.wordpress.com/2012/09/07/60-of-nurses-in-indias-biggest-hospital-are-victims-of-domestic-violence/

Aug 13, 2013, Kanpur: Woman allegedly commits suicide over dowry harassment. http://www.ndtv.com/article/cities/woman-allegedly-commits-suicide-over-dowry-harassment-405238

July 25, 2013, Ghazipur: 75 yr old and minor raped in separate incidents.
http://indianexpress.com/article/cities/lucknow/75yrold-minor-raped-in-separate-incidents/

July 19, 2013, India: Times Magazine, Every Two Hours in India, a Woman Dies From an Unsafe Abortion. http://world.time.com/2013/07/19/world-population-focus-on-india-part-2-unsafe-abortions/

July 09, 2013, Hyderabad: Former Andhra minister held in dowry harassment case. http://www.ndtv.com/article/south/former-andhra-minister-held-in-dowry-harassment-case-389585

June 27, 2013, Gujarat: Gujarat: 12,000 baby girls killed in the state's cities. http://www.asianews.it/news-en/Gujarat:-12,000-baby-girls-killed-in-the-state%27s-cities-28587.html

June 7, 2013, Barasat, West Bengal: Kamduni gang rape and murder case. http://en.wikipedia.org/wiki/2013_Kamduni_gang_rape_and_murder_case

May 19, 2013, Vijayawada, A.P.: Father tries to kill 3-day-old girl. http://timesofindia.indiatimes.com/city/hyderabad/Father-tries-to-kill-3-day-old-girl/articleshow/20128568.cms

Apr 20, 2013, Delhi: 5-yr-old rape survivor in ICU, family claims police acted late. http://ibnlive.in.com/news/delhi-5yrold-rape-survivor-in-icu-family-claims-police-acted-late/386373-3-244.html

March 30, 2013, Orissa: Former Odisha minister Raghunath Mohanty arrested in dowry case. http://www.ndtv.com/article/india/former-odisha-minister-raghunath-mohanty-arrested-in-dowry-case-348208 ; http://www.ndtv.com/article/india/former-odisha-minister-raghunath-mohanty-s-son-arrested-for-dowry-harassment-343448

March 18, 2013, Valsad: Probationary officer accuses bureaucrat husband of dowry harassment. http://www.ndtv.com/article/cities/probationary-officer-accuses-bureaucrat-husband-of-dowry-harassment-343953

March 17, 2013, Delhi: For conviction in dowry death, establish cruelty first: Supreme Court. http://www.ndtv.com/article/india/for-conviction-in-dowry-death-establish-cruelty-first-supreme-court-343539

January 28, 2013, Ludhiana: 'Duped' by NRI husband, Punjab woman files complaint. http://www.ndtv.com/article/cities/duped-by-nri-husband-punjab-woman-files-complaint-323211

January 7, 2013, Bombay: I Was Wounded; My Honour Wasn't. http://www.nytimes.com/2013/01/08/opinion/after-being-raped-i-was-wounded-my-honor-wasnt.html

January 15, 2013, Imphal: 2004 Manorama Devi rape-murder: No action against armed forces yet. http://ibnlive.in.com/news/2004-manorama-devi-rapemurder-no-action-against-armed-forces-yet/315794-3-225.html

Dec 22, 2012, Tamil Nadu: 13-year-old missing student found dead in Tamil Nadu. http://www.ndtv.com/article/south/13-year-old-missing-student-found-dead-in-tamil-nadu-308539 ; http://www.ndtv.com/article/south/13-year-old-missing-student-found-dead-cops-suspect-she-was-raped-before-murder-308225

Dec 12-16, 2012, Delhi: Nirbhaya, Delhi gang rape- Delhi Bus Gang Rape Victim Has Intestines Removed As Shocking Details Of Assault Emerge. http://www.huffingtonpost.com/2012/12/20/delhi-bus-gang-rape-victim-intestines-shocking-details_n_2340721.html ; http://ibnlive.in.com/news/delhi-gangrape-what-happened-on-the-night-of-december-16-2012/420729-3-244.html ; http://youtu.be/v5RbBXrdVPE ; http://en.wikipedia.org/wiki/2012_Delhi_gang_rape

Oct 28, 2012, Delhi: Minor girl murdered in Delhi, body dumped in
bin. http://www.ndtv.com/article/cities/minor-girl-murdered-in-delhi-body-dumped-in-bin-285388

Oct 18, 2012, Lakhimpur U.P.: Girl found dead in hostel
room. http://www.ndtv.com/article/cities/girl-found-dead-in-hostel-room-281284

Oct 1, 2012, Bhopal: Bhopal teen found raped,
murdered. http://www.ndtv.com/article/cities/bhopal-teen-found-raped-murdered-274335

Sep 27, 2012, Indore: Five-year-old girl dies under mysterious
circumstances. http://www.ndtv.com/article/cities/five-year-old-girl-dies-under-mysterious-circumstances-272997

Sep 02, 2012, Pune, Maharashtra: HC judge tells abused wife to
adjust. http://mobilepaper.timesofindia.com/mobile.aspx?article=yes&pageid=4&sectid=edid=
&edlabel=PMIR&mydateHid=02-09-2012&pubname=Mirror+-
+Pune&edname=&articleid=Ar00400&publabel=MM; http://indianhomemaker.wordpress.com/
2012/09/02/ask-your-father-if-he-has-never-beaten-your-mother-please-
adjust/; http://violenceonindianwomen.wordpress.com/2012/09/07/indian-judge-advices-
battered-wife-to-adjust-to-her-abuse/#more-412

Aug 29, 2012, India: Jawan's tonsure torture leaves wife
scared. http://www.newindianexpress.com/states/tamil_nadu/article597455.ece ; Read
more: http://masessaynotosexism.wordpress.com/2012/08/27/mother-and-daughter-tortured-
in-a-naked-manner-by-own-brothers/

Aug 24, 2012, Haryana: Woman injured in acid attack by
parents. http://ibnlive.in.com/news/haryana-woman-injured-in-acid-attack-by-parents/284973-
3-240.html

Aug 20, 2012, Ranchi: 'Reds' attack and shoot 4 women for not paying
'levy'. http://timesofindia.indiatimes.com/city/ranchi/Reds-attack-4-women-for-not-paying-
levy/articleshow/15564762.cms?referral=PM

Aug 13, 2012, Kashmir: Kashmiri Women Threatened With Acid Attack Violence For Not
Wearing Veils. http://www.ibtimes.com/kashmiri-women-threatened-acid-attack-violence-not-
wearing-veils-742935

Aug 13, 2012, Ranchi: Woman attacked with acid after refusing to have
sex. http://www.deccanherald.com/content/271289/woman-attacked-acid-refusing-have.html

Aug 11, 2012, Jaipur: Newborn girl found partly buried in farm,
survives. http://timesofindia.indiatimes.com/city/jaipur/Newborn-girl-found-partly-buried-in-
farm-survives/articleshow/15442387.cms?referral=PM

Aug 11, 2012, Delhi: Girl gang-raped by 8 men, dumped near Agra
highway. http://timesofindia.indiatimes.com/city/delhi/Girl-gang-raped-by-8-men-dumped-
near-Agra-highway/articleshow/15441784.cms?referral=PM

Aug 10-11, 2012, Mumbai: Guard killed advocate Pallavi after failed rape attempt.
http://www.hindustantimes.com/india-news/mumbai/guard-killed-pallavi-after-failed-rape-
attempt-cops/article1-911520.aspx
http://www.hindustantimes.com/india-news/mumbai/guard-killed-pallavi-after-failed-rape-
attempt-cops/article1-911520.aspx

Aug 10, 2012, Meerut: Woman patient alleges rape by two
doctors. http://www.ndtv.com/article/cities/woman-patient-alleges-rape-by-two-doctors-
253369

Aug 10, 2012, Lucknow, Uttar Pradesh: Hung up on 'honour', father murders girl who eloped. http://www.deccanherald.com/content/270779/hung-up-honour-father-murders.html

Aug 10, Jaisalmer, Rajasthan: Woman beaten up, burnt to death for dowry. http://timesofindia.indiatimes.com/city/jaipur/Woman-beaten-up-burnt-to-death-for-dowry/articleshow/15429770.cms?referral=PM

Aug 9, 2012, Vadodara, Gujarat: Woman killed – burnt alive – for alleged witchcraft. http://www.ucanindia.in/news/woman-killed-for-alleged-witchcraft/18753/daily

Aug 09, 2012, Chennai, Tamil Nadu: Mother tries to trow infant off a train, due to the child's gender. http://www.newindianexpress.com/cities/chennai/article585879.ece

Aug 7, 2012, Kolkata, West Bengal: Three held for forcing woman to foetus sex test and torturing her for refusal. http://www.newstrackindia.com/newsdetails/2012/08/07/424–Three-held-for-forcing-woman-to-foetus-sex-test-.html
Aug 7, 2012, Ranchi, Bihar: Posters warn women of acid attack for wearing jeans. http://www.deccanherald.com/content/269850/posters-warn-women-acid-attack.html

Aug 4, 2012, Jaipur, Bikaner: Parents prevent girl from studies, girl kills herself. http://timesofindia.indiatimes.com/city/jaipur/Denied-studies-girl-kills-herself/articleshow/15346098.cms

Aug 4, 2012, Jaipur, Rajasthan: 65-year-old woman beaten up and labelled 'witch'. http://violenceonindianwomen.wordpress.com/2012/08/16/65-year-old-woman-labelled-a-witch-and-beaten-up/

Aug 1, 2012, Berhampur: Forced abortion costs woman's life. http://www.newindianexpress.com/states/odisha/article580771.ece

Aug 1, 2012, Lucknow: 2 more cases of rape in 24 hours. http://timesofindia.indiatimes.com/city/lucknow/2-more-cases-of-rape-in-24-hours/articleshow/15300231.cms

Aug 1, 2012, Madurai: Doctor arrested for raping 16-year-old girl. http://ibnlive.in.com/news/doctor-held-for-raping-16yearold-girl/276888-62-128.html

July 31, 2012, Patna, Bihar: School Girl gang raped by a group of 8. http://timesofindia.indiatimes.com/city/patna/2-school-girls-gang-raped-in-Nalanda-district/articleshow/15287701.cms?referral=PM

July 27, 2012, Delhi: Disfigured victim's plea to die exposes India's acid violence. http://in.reuters.com/article/2012/07/27/india-acid-attacks-idINDEE86Q05420120727

July 27, 2012, Jagachha, West Bengal: Police unfazed with rape complaint. http://timesofindia.indiatimes.com/city/kolkata/Police-unfazed-with-rape-complaint/articleshow/15175762.cms?referral=PM ; http://violenceonindianwomen.wordpress.com/2012/08/01/police-and-hospital-turn-away-a-rape-victim/

July 26, 2012, Patna, Bihar: Patna girl raped by classmates, MMS circulated. http://ibnlive.in.com/news/patna-girl-raped-by-classmates-mms-circulated/274996-3-232.html ; http://violenceonindianwomen.wordpress.com/2012/08/01/school-girl-gang-raped-by-her-boyfriend-and-his-friends/

July 25, 2012, Goa: Raped Goa girl in critical condition after suicide attempt. http://archive.indianexpress.com/news/raped-goa-girl-in-critical-condition-after-suicide-attempt/979266/

July 18, 2012, Delhi: Dress carefully to avoid rape: NCW
chief. http://timesofindia.indiatimes.com/india/Dress-carefully-to-avoid-crime-NCW-
chief/articleshow/15036368.cms?
; http://violenceonindianwomen.wordpress.com/2012/07/19/chair-of-indias-national-
commission-for-women-says-clothing-invites-sexual-assault/

July 18, 2012, Indore, Madhya Pradesh: Indore man kept wife's private parts locked for four
years. http://archive.indianexpress.com/news/indore-man-kept-wifes-private-parts-locked-for-
four-years/976039/

July 13, 2012, Guwahati, Assam: Girl molested by mob, Assam CM calls for
action. http://ibnlive.in.com/news/guwahati-girl-molested-cm-calls-for-action/271180-3-
251.html ; http://violenceonindianwomen.wordpress.com/2012/07/14/teenage-girl-molested-
by-a-mob-of-20-men-in-full-public-view/

July 13, 2012, Hoogly, West Bengal: Inmates raped at will by outsiders in Hooghly
rehabilitation home. http://timesofindia.indiatimes.com/city/kolkata/Inmates-raped-at-will-by-
outsiders-in-Hooghly-rehabilitation-
home/articleshow/14857074.cms ; http://violenceonindianwomen.wordpress.com/2012/07/13/
men-allowed-to-rape-women-in-a-rehabiliation-home/

July 3, 2012, Sagar, Tyonda Village, Madhya Pradesh: Dowry case: Woman allegedly raped,
sold for Rs 50000. http://www.ndtv.com/article/india/dowry-case-woman-allegedly-raped-
sold-for-rs-50-000-239204

July 3, 2012, Noida: Dowry: Woman poisoned, kin block traffic with
body. http://timesofindia.indiatimes.com/city/noida/Dowry-Woman-poisoned-kin-block-traffic-
with-body/articleshow/14650121.cms?referral=PM

July 2, 2012, Malda, West Bengal: Man forces wife to drink acid in Malda.
http://timesofindia.indiatimes.com/city/kolkata/Man-forces-wife-to-drink-acid-in-
Malda/articleshow/14571742.cms?referral=PM

July 1, 2012, Guwahati, Assam: Woman MLA, who remarried without divorce, recounts horror
of mob attack in attempt of rape.
http://www.ndtv.com/article/india/woman-mla-who-remarried-without-divorce-recounts-horror-
of-mob-attack-238125 ; http://violenceonindianwomen.wordpress.com/2012/07/19/mob-
attacks-and-attempts-to-rape-a-female-politician/

June 30, 2012, Muzaffarnagar: Woman beaten to death for
dowry. http://www.ndtv.com/article/cities/woman-beaten-to-death-for-dowry-238031

June 27, 2012, India: Why are young Indians killing
themselves? http://www.bbc.com/news/world-asia-india-18592865

June 18, 2012, Jaisalmer: Parents adopt new methods to kill baby girls.
http://timesofindia.indiatimes.com/city/jaipur/Parents-adopt-new-methods-to-kill-baby-
girls/articleshow/14219200.cms?referral=PM; http://violenceonindianwomen.wordpress.com/2
012/06/28/indian-parents-are-plotting-their-daughters-murders-more-carefully/

June 16, 2012, Etah, U.P.: Woman, 2 daughters killed over dowry
demands. http://www.business-standard.com/article/pti-stories/woman-2-daughters-killed-
over-dowry-demands-112061600310_1.html

June 14, 2012, Delhi: Woman commits suicide in South Delhi, six held in dowry
case. http://www.ndtv.com/article/cities/woman-commits-suicide-in-south-delhi-six-held-in-
dowry-case-231575

June 12, 2012: Rita Banerji, 'India was rated as the worst country for women, ranking worse than Saudi Arabia.' http://violenceonindianwomen.wordpress.com/2012/06/22/india-worst-country-for-women-amgong-the-g20-nations/

June 11, 2012, Chennai: Posh south Chennai tops in dowry abuse cases. http://timesofindia.indiatimes.com/city/chennai/Posh-south-Chennai-tops-in-dowry-abuse-cases/articleshow/14007361.cms?referral=PM

June 7, 2012, Ahmadabad, Gujarat: 17-year-old girl commits suicide at Mahipatram Ashram. http://timesofindia.indiatimes.com/city/ahmedabad/17-year-old-girl-commits-suicide-at-Mahipatram-Ashram/articleshow/13877242.cms?referral=PM

June 6, 2012, Chandigarh: Haryana cops raped us: Children's home inmates. http://archive.indianexpress.com/news/haryana-cops-raped-us-childrens-home-inmates/958499/ ; http://violenceonindianwomen.wordpress.com/2012/06/07/minor-girls-in-indian-orphanage-raped-by-police/

May 27, 2012, 50 Million Missing: Kairi Sheperd: How An Adopted Indian Girl Is Now A Global Orphan. http://violenceonindianwomen.wordpress.com/2012/05/27/kairi-sheperd-how-an-adopted-indian-girl-is-now-a-global-orphan/

May 23, 2012, Beed, Maharashtra: Maharashtra: Doctors in Beed feed aborted female foetuses to dogs. http://indiatoday.intoday.in/story/doctors-in-beed-feed-aborted-female-foetuses-to-dogs/1/189919.html ; http://violenceonindianwomen.wordpress.com/2012/05/27/female-fetuses-fed-to-dogs-to-destroy-evidence-of-female-feticide/

May 22, 2012, Kanpur: Man and his mother get life term in dowry death – killing for a car. http://timesofindia.indiatimes.com/city/kanpur/Man-mother-get-life-term-in-dowry-death/articleshow/13374550.cms

May 22, 2012, Nagpur: Doctor arrested for dowry demands. http://timesofindia.indiatimes.com/city/nagpur/Doctor-booked-for-demanding-dowry/articleshow/13366881.cms?referral=PM

May 21, 2012, Delhi: Killed for dowry, dead woman's photo nails killers. http://www.financialexpress.com/news/killed-for-dowry-dead-womans-photo-nails-killers/952073/1

May 18, 2012, Hyderabad: Police Inspector arrested for dowry demands and harassments. http://ibnlive.in.com/news/cop-booked-for-dowry-harassment/259273-60-121.html

May 16, 2012, Gujarat: Police academy graduate accused of dowry demand. http://www.dnaindia.com/ahmedabad/report-police-academy-pass-out-accused-of-dowry-demand-1689484

May 12, 2012, Jharkhand, Bihar: Women killed by witchcraft. http://timesofindia.indiatimes.com/india/Witchcraft-claims-lives-of-four-women-in-Jharkhand/articleshow/13107605.cms?referral=PM

April 13, 2012, Punjab: Body of NRI's wife recovered from canal, police suspects dowry case. http://daily.bhaskar.com/article/PUN-OTC-body-of-nris-wife-recovered-from-canal-police-suspects-dowry-case-3085652.html

April 11, 2012, Bangalore: Baby Afreen breathes her last in hospital – killed by her father for being born a girl. http://www.deccanherald.com/content/241242/baby-afreen-breathes-her-last.html ; http://timesofindia.indiatimes.com/city/delhi/Baby-Falak-leaves-for-a-better-world/articleshow/12281081.cms?referral=PM ; http://violenceonindianwomen.wordpress.com/2012/04/12/baby-afreen-breathes-her-last-killed-by-her-dad-for-being-born-a-girl/

April 9, 2012, Kolkata, India: Constable sets son's wife ablaze for
dowry. http://archive.indianexpress.com/news/constable-sets-son-s-wife-ablaze-for-
dowry/934175/

April 9, 2012, Talcher: Man kills wife, injures mother-in-law.
http://ibnlive.in.com/news/dowry-man-kills-wife-injures-motherinlaw/247120-60-117.html

April 8, 2012, Lucknow: Major Dhyan Chand's granddaughter thrown out of home for
dowry. http://indiatoday.intoday.in/story/dowry-demon-torments-dhyan-chand-
grandkid/1/183490.html ; http://violenceonindianwomen.wordpress.com/2012/04/13/even-the-
known-and-famous-are-victims-of-dowry-abuse/

April 7, 2012, Gurdaspur: Woman kills daughter, sets herself
ablaze. http://ibnlive.in.com/generalnewsfeed/news/woman-kills-daughter-sets-herself-
ablaze/983807.html

April 6, 2012, Hydrabad: Man kills daughters to save dowry.
http://www.deccanherald.com/content/240232/man-kills-daughters-save-dowry.html

April 6, 2012, Bangalore: Woman commits suicide over
dowry. http://ibnlive.in.com/news/woman-commits-suicide-over-dowry/246263-60-119.html

April 3, 2012, Guntur A.P.: woman forced miscarriage for bearing girl
child. http://ibnlive.in.com/generalnewsfeed/news/ap-woman-forced-miscarriage-for-bearing-
girl-child/982416.html

March 31, 2012, Azamgarh: Pregnant girl found dead, mother
arrested. http://www.ndtv.com/article/cities/pregnant-girl-found-dead-mother-arrested-192350

March 25, 2012, Baharampur, West Bengal: Woman burnt to death for giving birth to
girls. http://ibnlive.in.com/news/wb-woman-burnt-to-death-for-giving-birth-to-girls/242589-
3.html

March 4, 2012: Revealed: The best and worst places to be a woman – Best place to drive a
car: India. http://www.independent.co.uk/news/world/politics/revealed-the-best-and-worst-
places-to-be-a-woman-7534794.html

Feb 25, 2012, Nadia: 8-yr jail term for dowry
death. http://timesofindia.indiatimes.com/city/kolkata/8-yr-jail-term-for-dowry-
death/articleshow/12027675.cms

Feb 24, 2012, Delhi: New-born girl's body found in west Delhi garbage
dump. http://www.ndtv.com/article/cities/new-born-girl-s-body-found-in-west-delhi-garbage-
dump-179246

Feb 24, 2012, Rourkela: 4 arrests in 2 dowry torture cases.
http://zeenews.india.com/news/odisha/4-arrests-in-2-dowry-torture-cases_760295.html

Feb 24, 2012, Hydrabad: 9 murder-accused acquitted. http://ibnlive.in.com/news/9-
murderaccused-acquitted/233229-60-121.html

Feb 8, 2012, Bangalore: Two persons ended their lives in two separate
accidents. http://www.ndtv.com/article/karnataka/two-persons-ended-their-lives-in-two-
separate-accidents-174168

Jan 19, 2012, Mainpuri: Four of family get rigorous life imprisonment.
http://zeenews.india.com/news/uttar-pradesh/four-of-family-get-rigorous-life-
imprisonment_753583.html

Jan 19, 2012, Mumbai: Protest in Mumbai over three-year-old found dead in garbage. http://www.ndtv.com/article/cities/protest-in-mumbai-over-three-year-old-found-dead-in-garbage-168601

Jan 17, 2012, Bhubaneshwar: Female Forest Service (OFS) officer alleges cop inaction against hubby. http://timesofindia.indiatimes.com/city/bhubaneswar/Harassed-officer-alleges-cop-inaction-against-hubby/articleshow/11517188.cms?referral=PM

Jan 10, 2012, Cuttak: 20-yr-old girl found dead near college hostel. http://www.ndtv.com/article/cities/20-yr-old-girl-found-dead-near-college-hostel-165258

Dec 31, 2011, India: Crime Against Women. http://ncrb.nic.in/CD-CII2011/cii-2011/Chapter%205.pdf

Dec 23, 2011, Ghaziabad: 20-year-old girl found dead, dishonour killing suspected. http://www.ndtv.com/article/cities/20-year-old-girl-found-dead-dishonour-killing-suspected-160143

Dec 20, 2011 & Jan 10, 2010, Save Indian family Foundation: President of India's kin in dowry trouble. http://www.saveindianfamily.org/blogs/prez-kin-in-dowry-trouble/3009 ; http://violenceonindianwomen.wordpress.com/2011/12/22/relative-of-indias-president-under-dowry-harassment-investigation/

Dec 19, 2011, Mumbai: Doc arrested over Rs 2 lakhs dowry demand. http://archive.mid-day.com/news/2011/dec/191211-Doc-arrested-over-Rs-2-lakh-dowry-demand.htm

Dec 16, 2011, Jaipur: Australian girl found dead in Jaipur hotel. http://www.ndtv.com/article/jaipur/australian-girl-found-dead-in-jaipur-hotel-158252

Dec 13, 2011, Delhi: Four-year-old girl raped by elderly man. http://www.ndtv.com/article/cities/four-year-old-girl-raped-by-elderly-man-157426

Dec 11, 2011, Mumbai: Hubby, in-laws booked for 51L dowry demand. http://timesofindia.indiatimes.com/city/mumbai/Hubby-in-laws-booked-for-51L-dowry-demand/articleshow/11065460.cms

Dec 3, 2011, Banka: Husband, father-in-law sentenced to life in a dowry death case. http://ibnlive.in.com/generalnewsfeed/news/husband-fatherinlaw-sentenced-to-life-in-a-dowry-death-case/921818.html

Nov 29, 2011, Noida: Nisha Sharma dowry case in final stage. http://www.hindustantimes.com/India-news/UttarPradesh/Nisha-Sharma-dowry-case-in-final-stage/Article1-775324.aspx

Nov 26, 2011, Madurai: Girl commits suicide due to dowry demand. http://timesofindia.indiatimes.com/city/madurai/Girl-commits-suicide-due-to-dowry-demand/articleshow/10876251.cms?referral=PM

Nov 24, 2011, Andhra Pradesh: Woman bleeds to death after forced abortion in Andhra Pradesh http://indiatoday.intoday.in/story/woman-bleeds-to-death-after-forced-abortion/1/161334.html

Nov 24, 2011, Delhi: Schoolteacher denied bail in dowry death case. http://zeenews.india.com/news/delhi/school-teacher-denied-bail-in-dowry-death-case_743615.html

Nov 24, 2011, Andhra Pradesh: Woman bleeds to death after forced abortion in Andhra Pradesh. http://indiatoday.intoday.in/story/woman-bleeds-to-death-after-forced-abortion/1/161334.html

Nov 21, 2011, Bangalore: Dowry: Newly-wed woman ends life. http://ibnlive.in.com/news/dowry-newlywed-woman-ends-life/204363-60-119.html

Nov 21, 2011, Pakur, Jharkhand: Nun killed by men of her group, say police; 7 held. http://archive.indianexpress.com/news/nun-killed-by-men-of-her-group-say-police;-7-held/878460/

Nov 17, 2011, Delhi: Army official wanted in dowry case surrenders in Chandigarh. http://indiatoday.intoday.in/story/army-major-dowry-case-chandigarh-police/1/160343.html

Nov 10, 2011, India: 13-Year-Old Tribal Girl Raped By The Headmaster. http://www.scoop.co.nz/stories/WO1111/S00253/india-13-year-old-tribal-girl-raped-by-the-headmaster.htm

Oct 30, 2011, Delhi: Youth gets 10-year prison term for raping minor girl. http://archive.indianexpress.com/news/youth-gets-10year-prison-term-for-raping-minor-girl/867709/

Oct 28, 2011, Bhaghpat, Uttar Pradesh: Modern Age Draupadi, Wife-sharing haunts Indian villages as girls decline. http://www.moneycontrol.com/news/current-affairs/wife-sharing-haunts-indian-villages-as-girls-decline_606255.html?utm_source=ref_article

Oct 20, 2011, Bicholim: Husband held for dowry death at Bicholim. http://timesofindia.indiatimes.com/city/goa/Husband-held-for-dowry-death-at-Bicholim/articleshow/10421661.cms?referral=PM

Oct 10, 2011, U.P.: Wealthy UP family parades Dalit woman naked. https://in.news.yahoo.com/wealthy-up-family-parades-dalit-woman-naked.html

Oct 7, 2011, Bhopal: Newborn girl found buried alive on the 2nd day of Beti Bachao Abhiyan in MP. http://post.jagran.com/newborn-girl-found-buried-alive-on-the-2nd-day-of-beti-bachao-abhiyan-in-mp-1318011451

Oct 3, 2011, Nashik: Woman arrested for allegedly killing her infant daughter. http://www.ndtv.com/article/cities/woman-arrested-for-allegedly-killing-her-infant-daughter-138175

Oct 2, 2011, India: Dowry murders – 106000 women burnt to death in 1 year. http://genderbytes.wordpress.com/2011/10/02/video-murder-by-fire-100000-women-a-year/

Oct 1-3, 2011, Kanpur: 25-yr-old pregnant woman killed for dowry. http://timesofindia.indiatimes.com/city/kanpur/25-yr-old-pregnant-woman-killed-for-dowry/articleshow/10192195.cms?referral=PM ; http://www.dnaindia.com/mumbai/report-pregnant-woman-murdered-for-dowry-by-husband-in-laws-1594613

Sep 26, 2011, Patna: Amrita Kumari was thrown off Patna's Gandhi Setu for dowry. http://www.iamnirbhaya.me/reports/view/350; http://violenceonindianwomen.wordpress.com/2011/09/26/amrita-kumaris-attempted-gang-murder-for-dowry/

Sep 24, 2011, Saharanpur: Woman killed for giving birth to girl. http://www.saharasamay.com/regional-news/uttar-pradesh-news/676493803/woman-killed-for-giving-birth-to-girl.html

Sep 22, 2011, Mahbubnagar, Andhra Pradesh: Woman kills herself, and kids, over dowry torture. http://timesofindia.indiatimes.com/city/hyderabad/Woman-kills-kids-self-over-dowry-torture/articleshow/10073799.cms?referral=PM

Sep 14, 2011, Ghaziabad: Woman set on fire for giving birth to girl. http://archive.indianexpress.com/news/woman-set-on-fire-for-giving-birth-to-girl/846657/

Sep 13, 2011, Bangalore: Support to wife-beater Darshan exposes our warped value system. http://www.dnaindia.com/entertainment/report-support-to-wife-beater-darshan-exposes-our-warped-value-system-1586637

Aug 30, 2011, Mumbai: Mumbai pilot arrested at airport for abusing wife. http://www.ndtv.com/article/cities/mumbai-pilot-arrested-at-airport-for-abusing-wife-130037

Aug 18, 2011, Alur, Karnataka: Dowry: Woman killed by hubby. http://www.deccanherald.com/content/89730/dowry-woman-killed-hubby.html

Aug 10, 2011, Hyderabad: Honour killing: Father kills daughter. http://ibnlive.in.com/news/honour-killing-father-kills-daughter/174452-60-121.html

July 13, 2011, Kendrapa: Cop kills wife for dowry. http://www.telegraphindia.com/1110714/jsp/orissa/story_14234726.jsp

July 5, 2011, Chandigarh: Father to Killer, Teen killed for rejecting 50-yr-old groom. http://news.oneindia.in/2011/07/05/father-kills-girl-for-rejecting-50-yr-old-groom-haryana-aid0101.html

Jun 15, 2011: The Guardian, Afghanistan worst place in the world for women, but India in top five. http://www.theguardian.com/world/2011/jun/15/worst-place-women-afghanistan-india

Jun 13, 2011: G20 countries: the worst and best for women. http://www.trust.org/spotlight/G20-Countries-the-worst-and-best-for-women/

June 11, 2011, India: Why Genocidal Violence on Women in India Increases with Wealth and Education https://genderbytes.wordpress.com/2011/06/12/why-education-and-economics-are-not-the-solution-to-indias-female-genocide/

June 07, 2011, Bangalore: Software firm employee booked in dowry death case. http://www.ndtv.com/article/cities/software-firm-employee-booked-in-dowry-death-case-110607

June 4, 2011, Mumbai: Girl, grandmother found dead at Antop Hill. http://www.ndtv.com/article/cities/girl-grandmother-found-dead-at-antop-hill-110064

June 1, 2011, Jaipur: FIR against villagers for branding woman witch'. http://timesofindia.indiatimes.com/city/jaipur/FIR-against-villagers-for-branding-woman-witch/articleshow/8670858.cms?referral=PM

May 23, 2011, Rajahmundry/Amalapuram: Man slits throat, hands of wife. http://timesofindia.indiatimes.com/india/Man-slits-throat-hands-of-wife/articleshow/8509606.cms?referral=PM

May 21, 2011, Raipur, India: Gang blinds Indian woman, accused of witchcraft, with scissors. http://www.reuters.com/article/2011/05/21/us-india-attack-witchcraft-idUSTRE74K0WY20110521

Apr 19, 2011, Mumbai: Dowry drives HDFC bank manager to
suicide. http://daily.bhaskar.com/article/MAH-MUM-dowry-drives-hdfc-manager-to-suicide-
2032498.html

Apr 7, 2011, Ahmadabad: Infant girl killed before being
dumped. http://timesofindia.indiatimes.com/city/ahmedabad/Infant-girl-killed-before-being-
dumped/articleshow/7889069.cms?referral=PM

Mar 20, 2011, Bangalore: Mother killed daughter,
grandchild. http://timesofindia.indiatimes.com/city/bangalore/Mother-killed-daughter-
grandchild/articleshow/7745568.cms?referral=PM

Mar 15, 2011, Surat: Body of 4-year-old missing girl found from closed
house. http://www.ndtv.com/article/cities/body-of-4-year-old-missing-girl-found-from-closed-
house-91894

Feb 21, 2011, Chennai: Why are Indian women setting themselves on
fire? http://violenceonindianwomen.wordpress.com/2011/08/18/why-are-indian-women-
setting-themselves-on-fire/#more-5

Jan 30, 2011, Mumbai: Three-year-old girl found dead inside
gutter. http://www.ndtv.com/article/cities/three-year-old-girl-found-dead-inside-gutter-82354

Jan 25, 2011, Jaipur: Newborn girl killed in
Rajasthan. http://www.facenfacts.com/NewsDetails/4004/newborn-girl-killed-in-rajasthan.htm

Dec 26, 2010, Rohtak: Father allegedly kills daughter, honour killing
suspected. http://timesofindia.indiatimes.com/india/Father-allegedly-kills-daughter-honour-
killing-suspected/articleshow/7166625.cms?referral=PM

October 25, 2010, Ahmadabad: Body of 20-year-old girl found in
sewer. http://www.ndtv.com/article/cities/body-of-20-year-old-girl-found-in-sewer-62075

June 30, 2010, Delhi: Delhi girl alleges physical assault at late night
party. http://www.ndtv.com/article/cities/delhi-girl-alleges-physical-assault-at-late-night-party-
34736

June 28, 2010, Delhi: 27-year-old girl found dead in rented flat.
http://www.ndtv.com/article/cities/delhi-27-year-old-girl-found-dead-in-rented-flat-34392

May 8, 2010, Koderma, Delhi: Nirupama's boyfriend is charged with
rape. http://www.ndtv.com/article/india/nirupama-s-boyfriend-is-charged-with-rape-23950

March 16, 2010, Mumbai: Child found dead floating in temple's water
tank. http://www.ndtv.com/article/cities/child-found-dead-floating-in-temple-s-water-tank-
17846

March 7, 2010, Mumbai: Girl found dead in police quarters.
http://www.ndtv.com/article/cities/mumbai-girl-found-dead-in-police-quarters-17326

Oct 9, 2009, Madurai: Infanticide in Tamil Nadu: Twin girls
killed. http://timesofindia.indiatimes.com/india/Infanticide-in-Tamil-Nadu-Twin-girls-
killed/articleshow/5103288.cms?referral=PM

Jun 26, 2009, Ludhiana: Woman 'killed' for giving birth to baby
girl. http://timesofindia.indiatimes.com/city/ludhiana/Woman-killed-for-giving-birth-to-baby-
girl/articleshow/4707672.cms?referral=PM

May 20, 2009, Bhatinda: Woman dies during forced abortion of female
fœtus. http://epaper.timesofindia.com/Repository/ml.asp?Ref=Q0FQLzlwMDkvMDUvMjAjQXl
wMTkwMQ==&Mode=HTML&Locale=english-skin-custom

Dec 20, 2008, Chhattisgarh: Man deserts wife for giving birth to
daughter. http://www.dnaindia.com/india/report-man-deserts-wife-for-giving-birth-to-daughter-
1215549

March 7, 2008, Burdwan, West Bengal: Daughters drowned, to escape
'taunts'. http://www.telegraphindia.com/1080307/jsp/bengal/story_8991182.jsp

Dec 24, 2007, New Delhi: 1 dowry death every 4 hrs in India.
http://zeenews.india.com/home/1-dowry-death-every-4-hrs-in-india_414869.html

Oct 19, 2007, Amravati: Woman killed for giving birth to girl in
Amravati. http://timesofindia.indiatimes.com/city/nagpur/Woman-killed-for-giving-birth-to-girl-
in-Amravati/articleshow/2472243.cms?referral=PM

Jul 24, 2007, Ahmedabad: 'Female foetus was buried for Rs
100'. http://timesofindia.indiatimes.com/city/ahmedabad/Female-foetus-was-buried-for-Rs-
100/articleshow/2228533.cms?referral=PM

May 31, 2006, India: One rape every half-hour in India; a dowry death every 75
minutes. http://infochangeindia.org/women/news/one-rape-every-half-hour-in-india-a-dowry-
death-every-75-minutes.html

Feb 8, 2006, Mother kills 1-day-old baby girl by
strangulation. http://expressindia.indianexpress.com/news/fullstory.php?newsid=62550

Sep 17 – 19, 2004, India Seminar, Germany: Girls, Mothers, Dowry: The women in India in
church and society.
http://ems-
online.org/fileadmin/_migrated/content_uploads/Dokubrief_Indien6_05_Englisch_02.pdf

June 25, 2004, Hydrabad: Andhra girl killed in US.
http://www.telegraphindia.com/1040625/asp/nation/story_3413141.asp

August 15, 2003, Bulandshahr: Lovers killed by parents.
http://timesofindia.indiatimes.com/city/delhi/Lovers-killed-by-parents/articleshow/132505.cms?